W9-AQU-317

MACAULAY'S

ESSAY ON WARREN HASTINGS

Macmillan's Pocket American and English Classics

A SERIES OF ENGLISH TEXTS, EDITED FOR USE IN ELEMENTARY AND SECONDARY SCHOOLS, WITH CRITICAL INTRODUCTIONS, NOTES, ETC.

Macmillan's Pocket American and English Classics

A SERIES OF ENGLISH TEXTS, EDITED FOR USE IN ELEMENTARY AND SECONDARY SCHOOLS, WITH CRITICAL INTRODUCTIONS, NOTES, ETC.

MACAULAY'S ESSAY

ON

WARREN HASTINGS

EDITED

WITH INTRODUCTION AND NOTES

BY

MRS. MARGARET J. FRICK

*Head of English Department, Los Angeles High
School, California*

New York

THE MACMILLAN COMPANY

LONDON: MACMILLAN & CO., Ltd.

1920

Copyright, 1900,

By THE MACMILLAN COMPANY.

CONTENTS

vii

4039

INTRODUCTION

LIFE OF MACAULAY

MACAULAY in one of his letters quotes the *Spectator* as observing, "We never read an author with much zest, unless we are acquainted with his surroundings." Many writers seem forced to give us their "circumstances" in their writings. Macaulay does not. He was never limited by his environment. In all the volumes given to the public by this most versatile writer, we can scarcely find a hint of his own character and surroundings. It is in his private letters and diary only that he freely gives us his personal life. From these we may trace the growth of the man. Never was there a life more completely self-directed than Macaulay's, nor a success more surely earned.

A short biography can do little more than refer to the logical growth of his greatness: his enthusiastic literary work; the high character that gave him entrance to Parliament, the quick grasp of public questions, and the far-seeing, honorable stand that made

him so powerful while there and led to his appointment in India; the unremitting application and
clear strength of mind that made his criminal code
for India a blessing to millions of people. Still less
can it tell how, during the twenty years of his busy
life as a leader in Parliament and in the midst of his
endless administration of duties in India, he always
found time to entertain his friends, to read the classics
of many lands in the native tongues, and to write
thousands of pages of essays, poetry, and history.
This sketch aims merely at giving an impression of
some of the characteristics of the man and an outline
of the most important events of his career.   One
desiring to study more fully his admirable life and
character will enjoy *Macaulay's Life and Letters*, a
collection of his letters, extracts from his diary, and
letters to him, edited by Otto Trevelyan, the son of his
sister Hannah.

Thomas Babington Macaulay was born at Rothley
Temple, Leicestershire, October 25, 1800. His great-
grandfather and grandfather were Scotch ministers.
From them he seems to have inherited, among other
honest opinions, their personal creed that they " had
no notion of people being in earnest in good profes-
sions if their practice belied them."   His father,
Zachary Macaulay, was a quiet, stern man of very
strong political convictions and absolutely disinter-

ested adherence to them. A brief residence in Jamaica in his youth had acquainted him with the cruelties practised on the slaves there. After his return to England, through the columns of the *Christian Observer*, of which he was editor, he labored earnestly to force legislation to free the slaves of the West Indies. This brought him into close association with Wilberforce and other political reformers who were working for the same end. His home was a centre for consultation for the members of Parliament who lived on the Surrey side of London. Thus young Macaulay was admitted to the intimacy of politicians while he was still a child, and was made familiar with the workings of Parliament. His mother gave the boy the love and petting his affectionate nature craved, and she recognized the unusual activity of his mind. How could any mother be blind to the precocity of a child of three years who spent his happiest hours lying before the fire with a piece of bread and butter in his hand, reading from a book open before him on the rug; and who, when eight years old, had memorized all of Scott's *Lay of the Last Minstrel* and *Marmion*, unconsciously, simply through the delight in reading them? Fortunately for him both his father and his mother had the wisdom to refrain from parading his accomplishments, and they insisted on a like treatment from their friends and the child's tutors. There were eight other children, three brothers and five sisters. Thomas was the eldest, and the idol of all the rest. He was the sunshine of the family, they said, and when Tom was away there was never any fun at all, or anything worth doing.

Hannah More may be regarded as his first literary patron. She treated him as a child, but rewarded his poetic efforts by presenting to him his first books to start a library. His first hero was his uncle, General Colin Macaulay, who was retired from service in India. This nephew of ten evidently desired more fighting for his hero, for he hinted in verse : —

> " For many a battle shall be lost and won,
>   Ere yet thy glorious labors shall be done."

When Macaulay was about thirteen years old he was sent from home to a private school. At this time begins the long series of letters which serve to make up the real biography of his life. These first letters tell of his studies and his readings, and many of them disclose the intense homesickness of this home-loving boy. In one addressed to his mother he writes: "Everything I read or hear or see brings home to my mind. You told me I should be happy when I once came here, but not an hour passes in which I do not shed tears at thinking of home. Tell me in your next, expressly, if you can, whether or no there is any likelihood of my coming home before the holidays; if your approbation of my request depends upon my advancing in study I will work like a cart-horse."

In 1818 he entered Trinity College, Cambridge. There his love of literature and his vivid interest in outside political affairs seem fairly balanced. He took many prizes, but lost many that others thought he deserved. The losses he seems to have taken philosophically, for in later years he wrote, "If a man brings away from Cambridge self-knowledge, accuracy of mind, and habits of strong intellectual exertion, he has gained more than if he had made a display and show of superficial scholarship; for, after all, what a man does at Cambridge is in itself nothing." He took his A.B. degree in 1822, and was elected to a fellowship in Trinity in 1824. Two changes had come to him while he was in college. When he entered, his father was in affluent circumstances. By mismanagement somewhere the business in which the money was invested failed. Thomas and his brother Henry ultimately paid off the father's debts, but upon Thomas fell the support of the family. While waiting for his fellowship he did some tutoring. When the fellowship came, its three hundred pounds a year, with about three hundred that he made by his writing, enabled the family to live happily, if not luxuriously. Of his assuming this charge his biog-

rapher says: "He quietly took up the burden which
his father was unable to bear, and before many years
had elapsed the fortunes of all for whose welfare
he considered himself responsible were abundantly
assured. In the course of the efforts which he expended on the accomplishment of this result he unlearned the very notion of framing his method of
life with a view to his own pleasure; and such was
his high and simple nature that it may well be
doubted whether it ever crossed his mind that to live
wholly for others was a sacrifice at all." His sister's
tribute is, "Those were years of intense happiness;
if there were money troubles, they did not touch us.
We traversed every part of the city, Islington, Clerk-
enwell, and the parks, returning just in time for a six
o'clock dinner. What anecdotes he used to pour out
about every street and court and square and alley!
Then after dinner he always walked up and down the
drawing-room between us, chatting till tea-time. Our
noisy mirth, his wretched puns, so many a minute,
so many an hour!"

The other change was of political opinion. He,
like his father, was a Tory, but before the end of his
first year at Cambridge he had been converted to
Whig principles. It was a time of extreme views,
when riots were occurring in all the large cities; the
cry was "Bread or Blood," and the famous "Six Acts"

had been passed; but though Macaulay had always been a reformer and had now turned Whig, his mind was cool and well balanced, so that at no time was he a revolutionist.

It was during his college life that his contributions to *Knight's Quarterly Magazine* began. These earliest writings show the essential features of that direct, lucid "style" which has since come to be famous. *The Battle of Ivry*, *The Battle of Naseby*, and *The Conversation of Mr. Abraham Cowley and Mr. John Milton touching the Great Civil War* were published in this magazine. His father disapproved of such light literature as poetry and essays, and he very strongly disapproved of *Knight's Quarterly Magazine*. Macaulay's answers to his father's letters of remonstrance are gentle and respectful. Occasionally, though, he breaks forth, as in one letter: "Consistency with a vengeance! The reading of modern poetry and novels is complained of as exciting a worldly disposition and preventing ladies from reading Dryden's Fables!" Still, the disapproval of those he loved pained him, and it must have been relief as well as pride that made him promise his father a "piece of secret history." The editors of the *Edinburgh Review*, a liberal publication which wielded the greatest power in social, political, and literary circles, had been looking about for a new writer who should be young, clever, and not a Tory. Macaulay's writings in *Knight's Quarterly Magazine* attracted them, and the "piece of secret history" was the news of an invitation from the editors of the *Edinburgh Review* to write for them.

His first contribution, the essay on Milton, made him famous. Its very youthful exuberance of enthusiasm for Milton, whom he loved and admired, was warmly welcomed by the friends of the great poet, for they felt the need at that time of some appreciative partisan to contest the harsh judgment set forth in Dr. Johnson's *Life of Milton*. We still read and admire this brilliant essay, but it is only by remembering the lack of popular reading in Macaulay's time and comparing this essay on Milton with the other essays and biographies of the day that we can understand the surprise and pleasure it gave to the reading public. The grudging compliment of Jeffrey, the reviewer, "The more I think, the less I can conceive where you picked up that style!" shows the impression it made on the critics. From the publication of the *Milton* in 1825 Macaulay was for twenty years a steady contributor to the *Edinburgh Review*. In it were first published over forty of his best-known poems and essays, written regularly through all the years that were apparently full of the public duties of a member of Parliament.

Macaulay was called to the bar in 1826, but took

little interest in law, preferring to spend his time under the gallery of the House of Commons. He seems always to have thrown all his tremendous energy into the subject in which he had a present interest, and he refused to dissipate his power even in what at times appeared to others as the things he ought to do. Thus at this time, when he was ostensibly preparing himself to be an advocate, he did little reading in law; but later, when he was sent to India and knew that he was to be a lawgiver there, he mastered on his voyage the necessary branches of the law in principle and minutest detail. One who knew him best said of him: "Throughout life he never really applied himself to any pursuit that was against the grain."

Though he had but little law practice, his fellowship, his writings for the *Edinburgh Review,* and the Commissionership of Bankruptcy that a friend had secured for him brought him almost one thousand pounds a year, sufficient for the needs of himself and the family, but no more. He was now thirty years old, and all his life he had had a keen interest in political questions. This was the exciting time of the "Rotten Boroughs," when the "Test Act" had just been repealed and the "Reform Bill" was seething, and it is not to be wondered at that Macaulay felt his strength and longed for an opportunity to take an active part;

but it seemed a hopeless longing, as he had no money to buy a seat in Parliament, and among politicians he was almost unknown. Fortunately his writings had made him a friend, Lord Lansdowne, who said: "The *Milton* and especially the articles on Mill have so impressed me that I wish to be the one to introduce their author to public life by offering him a seat in Parliament for the borough of Calne, and as it is his high moral and private character which has determined me to make the offer, I wish in no respect to influence his votes, but to leave him quite at liberty to act according to his conscience." So in 1830 the House of Commons received one of its great orators and far-seeing statesmen, and Macaulay's wish was gratified.

His first speech was in favor of removing all civil disabilities from the Jews. In this his maiden effort in Parliament he used with great skill his favorite device for overpowering an opponent. Placing his adversary's statements on one side of the scales, he heaps his own counter-statements and deductions on the other, until the listener or reader who is following his argument feels that Macaulay's side of the scales is weighted to the ground, while his opponent's is left in mid-air. This first speech called forth many compliments from the older members, which might have emboldened another man; but though Macaulay loved to talk he was too modest and had too much common sense to appear on the floor of the House unless his voice seemed to be needed.

His great opportunity arose in the very constitution of the House itself. The House of Commons was formed in the thirteenth century, the summons reading, "two knights from every shire," "two burgesses from every city, borough, and leading town." In the five hundred years since, no reorganization of the House had been made, though some of the boroughs that still sent representatives had lost all of their inhabitants, and other small boroughs had been created by sovereigns who needed votes in the House. On the other hand, many great cities had grown up in districts not provided for originally, and these masses of citizens were still unrepresented. In the eighteenth century such men as Chatham and Burke had worked on the problem of the reform of the House, until this subject had been crowded out by consideration of the troubles with France; but for ten years previous to Macaulay's coming to the House one reform bill after another had been brought forward and rejected. The country was demanding more and more urgently a change; but the Tory Ministry and the House of Lords with the unreformed House of Commons were against it.

At the beginning of Macaulay's second session in the House of Commons the Whigs were returned by a large majority, and the Tory Ministry was forced to resign. Under the new Whig Ministry Lord John Russell's Reform Bill came up. This bill gave a franchise to many hitherto unrepresented cities and boroughs; but the clause in it which disfranchised wholly or partially one hundred and ten boroughs was pronounced, by the leaders of the Opposition, so extravagant that they ridiculed any suggestion that the bill could be passed. March 2, 1831, Macaulay made the first of his speeches on this Reform Bill. As his *Milton* had won him immediate recognition as a literary man, so this speech gave him distinction at once among the orators and statesmen of England. The Speaker of the House sent for him and told him that he had never seen the House in such a state of excitement. Sir Robert Peel and Sir Thomas Denman complimented him in stately terms. But the greatest compliment paid to this and his following reform speeches was, that the leaders of the Opposition felt called upon to devote more time to answering his speeches than to attacking those of the older debaters. To Macaulay's great satisfaction this Reform Bill carried.

The following years he was, as he always had been, a strenuous worker. Besides his duties in the House he had other official duties, and his political honors had given him entrance to the best London society.

His letters give pictures of breathless pauses in the House till a majority of one sends them laughing, crying, and huzzaing into the lobby, or of such a state as this: "Toward eight in the morning the Speaker was almost fainting. . . . Old Sir Thomas Baring sent for his razor and Benett for his nightcap; they were both resolved to spend the whole day in the House rather than give way. If the Opposition had not yielded in two hours half of London would have been in Old Palace Yard." Other pictures he gives us of dinners with Lord Grey and Lord John Russell, of breakfasts in the beautiful home of Rogers the poet, of music parties where he heard the first flute player in England and "pianoforte strumming by the first pianoforte strummer," of meetings with Talleyrand and Sydney Smith, Tom Moore and Tom Campbell, and of innumerable courtesies from that haughty old aristocrat, Lady Holland. The political reward for Macaulay's services on the Reform Bill was an appointment on the Board of Control in the East India affairs.

In the midst of these social and political successes which he so frankly enjoyed, his simple creed of voting for the best interest of the country endured several severe tests. In each case he seems to have realized and deplored the consequences to himself, but did not allow them to influence his actions. His own vote

assisted in abolishing the office by which he held his
Commissionership of Bankruptcy, at a time when he
was not earning much by his writing and within a
few months of the expiration of his income from the
fellowship. A still stronger temptation to consider
self was withstood when he decided to send in his
resignation, so that he might go upon the floor of
the House and oppose a measure brought in by his
own party, a slavery bill that did not come up to the
rigid requirements of his father and other Abolitionists.
Trevelyan says: "During the crisis of the West India
Bill Zachary Macaulay and his son were in constant correspondence. There is something touching in the picture which these letters present of the older man (whose
years were coming to a close in poverty, which was the
consequence of his having always lived too much for
others), discussing quietly and gravely how and when
the younger was to take a step that in the opinion of
them both would be fatal to his career; and this with
so little consciousness that there was anything heroic
in the course which they were pursuing, that it appears
never to have occurred to either of them that any other
line of conduct could possibly be adopted." But Macaulay's honesty was appreciated and he writes jubilantly:
"Here I am safe and well at the end of one of the most
stormy weeks that the oldest man remembers in Parliamentary affairs. I have resigned my office and my

resignation has been refused. I have spoken and voted against the Ministry under which I hold my place." And again he writes: "I have, therefore, the singular good luck of having saved both my honor and my place."

In 1834 he was chosen by the government to go to Calcutta as their representative in the Supreme Council. To Lord Lansdowne, his friend and political patron, he told his reasons for accepting a position which seemed to all a sacrifice of his political ambitions. "Every day that I live, I become less and less desirous of great wealth. But every day makes me more sensible of the importance of a competence. Without a competence it is not easy for a public man to be honest; it is almost impossible for him to be thought so. I am so situated that I can subsist only in two ways: by being in office and by my pen. . . . The thought of becoming a book-seller's hack, of writing to relieve, not the fulness of the mind, but the emptiness of the pocket, . . . is horrible to me. Yet thus it must be if I should quit office. Yet to hold office merely for the sake of emolument would be more horrible still. . . . But this is not all. I am not alone in the world. A family which I love most fondly is dependent on me. . . . An opportunity has offered itself. . . . I may hope by the time I am thirty-nine or forty to return to England with a fortune of thirty thousand pounds. To me that would be affluence." On the first intimation of this offer he had written to his sister Hannah, telling her of the dignity and consideration attached to the post, and of the high salary, ten thousand pounds a year, and added: " Whether the period of my exile shall be one of comfort, and after the first shock, even of happiness, depends on you. If, as I expect, this offer shall be made to me, will you go with me ? I know what a sacrifice I ask of you. I know how many dear and precious ties you must, for a time, sunder. I know that the splendor of the Indian court, and the gayeties of that brilliant society of which you would be one of the leading personages, have no temptation for you. I can bribe you only by telling you that, if you will go with me, I will love you better than I love you now, if I can."

His preparations for the voyage to India were characteristic. He visited the ship to inspect the cabin his sister was to occupy, and ordered it to be made as pretty and comfortable as possible for the long voyage. He wrote to the publishers of the *Edinburgh Review* that he would continue to furnish articles to them, but he desired to be paid while in India with books. He gave his preference for books on English History, as he had already begun work on his own *History* at that time.

Among the books which he had provided for his own reading on the voyage were Voltaire's works, Gibbon, Sismondi's *History of the French, Don Quixote*

m Spanish, Homer in Greek, Horace in Latin, all the
Edinburgh Reviews bound, a collection of Greek classics, some books of jurisprudence, some to initiate him
in Persian and Hindoostanee, and his favorite novels.
He warned his sister that he had brought Gisborne's
Duties of Women, Moore's *Fables for the Female Sex*,
Mrs. K.'s *Female Scripture Characters* and Fordyce's
Sermons to keep her in order, — and then asked her to
tell him seriously what she would like to have. On
the voyage his letters tell that his sister danced with
the gentlemen in the evenings and read novels and
sermons with the ladies in the mornings; but that he
hardly spoke except at meals, keenly enjoying the
chance to be alone and, as he puts it, to "devour Greek,
Latin, Spanish, Italian, French, and English, — folios,
quartos, octavos, and duodecimos."

When the vessel touched at Madras Macaulay found
instructions awaiting him from Lord Bentinck, the
Governor-General of India, which required his leaving
the coast and travelling by palanquin to the Nilgiris
Hills, beyond Mysore. He was thus thrown at once
in contact with the natives. At Arcot he visited the
deserted gardens of the Nabob of the Carnatic; and
at Mysore he was received by the deposed Rajah,
whose palaces, furniture, jewels, soldiers, elephants,
and idols were subjects for home letters. He digressed
from the main road to visit the old town and fortress

of Seringapatam, a place having a double interest for him. He had been familiar with it from a child, through the stories told him by the hero uncle, General Macaulay, who had been imprisoned there for four years; and he was now interested in exploring the ruins of the splendid court and halls, and in seeing the great mausoleum within which are the tombs of Hyder Ali, Tippoo Sultan, and Tippoo's mother, all covered with palls embroidered in gold with verses from the Koran.

When he was relieved by Lord Bentinck he went on to Calcutta, and there he and sister Hannah went to housekeeping. Then began the unremitting grind of government administration which employed him during the entire time that he remained in India. He was made president of the Committee on Public Instruction for India, and we find him advocating teaching English in the schools, instead of Sanscrit, Persian, and Arabic, on the grounds of the value of English as a language, of the knowledge of the sciences that would come through it, and of its known civilizing effects. In this, as in other positions, he acquainted himself with the minutest details of the office for which he was responsible. He gave opinions on circulating libraries, qualifications of schoolmasters, the manner of awarding prizes, and on "public spouting in schools"; and made suitable lists of books for study and lists of books to be used for prizes. He was also made chairman of the Committee to draw up a Penal Code and Code of Criminal Procedure for India. Owing to the sickness of some of his colleagues most of the labor on the Penal Code fell to him. Of this remarkable code Mr. Fitzjames Stephens, a trained English lawyer and Macaulay's successor, says: "This Penal Code is to the English criminal law what a manufactured article ready for use is to the materials out of which it was made. It is to the French *Code Pénal*, and, I may add, to the North German Code of 1871, what a finished picture is to a sketch. The clearest proof of its practical success is that hardly any questions have arisen upon it which have had to be determined by the courts." The value of its plain instructions is most appreciated by those English magistrates who have been called upon to administer justice in a country where there is no common interpretation of the terms, crime and punishment.

At one time Macaulay was very unpopular in India. He had advocated an act which required that henceforth British subjects should bring civil appeals before the Sudder Court, instead of the Supreme Court of Council. His habitual fairness appears in this statement: "In my opinion the chief reason for preferring the Sudder Court is this, that it is the court which we have provided to administer justice, in the last resort,

to the great body of the people. . . . If we give our
own countrymen an appeal to the King's Courts, in
cases in which all others are forced to be contented
with the Company's Courts, we do in fact cry down the
Company's Courts. We proclaim to the Indian people
that there are two sorts of justice — a coarse one,
which we think good enough for them, and another of
superior quality, which we keep for ourselves." This
called down upon him such a storm of vituperation
from the Calcutta press that he was unwilling his
sister should see the papers. The abuse seems not to
have disturbed his equanimity in any other way, for
during these attacks he sent off a long state paper
setting forth his reasons for urging the removal of all
censorship from the press of India. By 1837 his
object in going to India had been attained, he had
acquired a fortune sufficient to allow him to reënter
political life or to retire and devote himself to writing. In a letter to a friend, he confessed his yearn-
ing for England. "Let me assure you," he wrote,
"banishment is no light matter." He left India in
December, 1837. On the voyage home he mastered
the German language, learning it as he had Spanish and Portuguese. His habit was to read first
the Bible in the new language, his familiarity with
the Bible making a dictionary unnecessary, then with
dictionary and grammar to attack some classical work.

Shortly after his return to England he began writing on his *History of England;* but his election to Parliament from Edinburgh, and the acceptance of a seat in the Cabinet, so interfered with this more exacting form of writing that he gave it up for a while, though he continued his contributions of book reviews, or essays, to the *Edinburgh Review* until 1844. His residence in India had attracted him to Indian subjects. He wrote to the *Edinburgh Review* that he would send them a life of Lord Clive. "The subject is a grand one, and admits of decorations and illustrations innumerable." Later he wrote: "I see that a life of Warren Hastings is just coming out. I mark it for mine." This refers to Gleig's *Life of Warren Hastings* that afterward furnished the materials, or rather the occasion, for the essay in this book on Warren Hastings.

From 1839 to 1847 Macaulay spoke on every important question that came up in Parliament. In 1847 he gave offence to his constituents of Edinburgh by some of his broad views, and he was not reëlected. He refused the offer of an election from another borough, welcoming his defeat because it gave him the needed time to devote to his *History of England.* The first two volumes were published in 1848. Their sale was phenomenal. He said of the *History,* "It is a work that never ceases and never presses." As he wrote the third and fourth volumes he became so absorbed that he gave up other writing except some articles for the *Encyclopedia Britannica*. The *History* had a more enthusiastic welcome than even he had hoped for it. Its sale in England outnumbered that of the popular novels. On the continent compliments and honors were showered upon him. From America Harper and Brothers wrote that the sixth edition was in the market, and no work of any kind had ever taken America so by storm.

In 1852 Macaulay was again returned to Parliament by the electors of Edinburgh at their own expense. He demonstrated by one brilliant effort that he had not lost his power, for the bill he opposed was "not thrown out, but pitched out." The strain of political life, however, was too great for him, as his health was failing, and in 1856 he applied for the Chiltern Hundreds.[1]

Many honors were conferred on the great man in his last years. He was elected Lord Rector of the

[1] By English law no member of Parliament is at liberty to resign his seat, so long as he is duly qualified; on the other hand a member who accepts an office under the crown must vacate his seat. A member desiring to resign, therefore, applies for the "Stewardship of the Chiltern Hundreds," an office formerly of importance, but now obsolete and merely nominal. The appointment necessitates his resignation as member of Parliament, and, having thus fulfilled its purpose, is again resigned, so as to be ready for the next member who wishes to use it.

University of Glasgow; made a Fellow of the Royal Society; elected a Foreign Member of the French Academy, and of the Prussian Order of Merit; and High Steward of Cambridge. He was raised to the peerage as Baron Macaulay of Rothley, the first literary man to receive this honor in recognition of literary work. And yet his last days were sad ones. He once said, " There are not ten people in the world whose deaths would spoil my dinner, but there are one or two whose deaths would break my heart." This " one or two " came to mean his sisters Margaret and Hannah. When Margaret died it did almost break his heart; and the marriage of his sister Hannah while he and she were in India seemed almost as hard to bear. His sister Hannah and her husband, Lord Trevelyan, were as devoted to him as he was to them, so they returned to England when he did and he lived with them or near them the remainder of his life. The year 1859 found him failing in bodily health very rapidly, although his friends did not know how ill he was. He continued to write on his *History*, but was sorrowfully conscious that he could not finish it. "To-day I wrote a pretty fair quantity of history. I should like to finish *William* before I go. But this is like the old excuses that were made to Charon."

A blow had fallen on him this year that probably hastened his end. His sister Hannah's husband had been appointed Governor of Madras, and had sailed for India; there the beloved Hannah must soon follow him. Macaulay accepted this, the heaviest trial that could come to him, with a cheerful acquiescence; but in his diary is the entry, " I could almost wish that what is to be were to be immediately. I dread the next four months more even than the months which will follow the separation. This prolonged parting — this slow sipping of the vinegar and the gall — is terrible."

As he grew weaker his anxiety lest he should grow irritable is expressed, and he adds, "But I will take care. I have thought several times of late that the last scene of the play is approaching. I should wish to act it simply, but with fortitude and gentleness united."

His wish was realized. His friends found him sitting in his easy chair in the library with his book open before him. The end had come before the dreaded parting from his sister.

He was buried in the Poets' Corner of Westminster Abbey on the 9th of January, 1860.

INDIA

When the British began trading in India they found the native people divided into two great contending forces — the Hindus and the Mohammedans. These two forces may be accounted for, in general, in this way, taking Sir William Wilson Hunter, a vice-president of the Royal Asiatic Society, as authority : —

The Hindus, made up of : —

Non-Aryans — (the Aborigines).

Aryans — (from Aryan plateau).

Scythians — (Huns, Tartars). (From Western Asia. Possibly non-Aryans, though probably Aryans.)

These three had formed a settled nation with a common religion; and their pride of birth, learning, and prowess had crystallized into the four great Hindu castes before the year 1000 A.D.

The Mohammedans.

About 1000 A.D. various Tartar tribes of Arabia, who had embraced Mohammedanism, overran India, conquering parts of it and setting up the Mogul Empire.

The Hindus : Non-Aryans. — Although the non-Aryans are called the Aborigines, the weapons and utensils of agate, flint, and iron that are found indicate earlier people than these, of whom there is no written account. The only history we have of the non-Aryans is in the Vedas of their conquerors, the Aryans. They have no race name. The Vedic poets sang of them as "the flat-nosed, black-skinned raw-eaters," and again, "of fearful swiftness, unyielding in battle, in color like a dark blue cloud." Their idols were hideous creatures whom they feared; they had no good deities. They are classed among the Hindus, but some of their tribes are scattered along the hills and mountains of India and retain distinctive tribe names. The Hillmen of Madras, the Bhils of the Vindya Hills, the Santals, and the Gurkhas of the Himalayas, are non-Aryans. These people are brave and loyal when fairly treated. The Gurkha regiments in the English army and the Bhil treasury-guards have justified the confidence placed in them.

THE ARYANS. — From the Aryan plateau in West Asia, branches of one great family set forth in different directions. Some travelled west and became what we know as the Greek and Roman nations, and from other branches that wandered on farther west we are descended through our Keltic and Teutonic fore-fathers. Still others went east and south. One entered the Punjab through the Himalayas and spread over India, conquering the non-Aryans or driving them to the mountains. Their earliest literature, the Rig-Veda, dated variously from 3000 to 1400 B.C., and their other Vedas, sing of their marching eastward and "subjecting the black-skinned to the Aryan man." These hymns praise the gods of the Aryan, "the Shining Ones," and condemn the hideous monsters of the Dasyus, or enemies. At first, like all conquering people, the Aryans confined themselves to war, and there seems to have been the same patriarchal form of government as in the Teutonic tribes. Gradually the people became divided into classes, through their occupations, and these classes are what are known to us as the castes of India, which are hereditary and whose bounds are impassable. For a time there seems to have been a struggle for supremacy between the soldier and student classes, which was won by the latter. The four great castes are the Brahman, Rajput, Vaisya, and Sudra: —

Brahmans. — The men of learning of India formed the highest caste. From this caste came the poets, philosophers, teachers, lawgivers, and priests of the people, but never the king. They were the advisers of the kings because they were the men of greatest wisdom, but it was not prudent that king and counsellors should all come from the same class, so the king was always one of the Rajputs. They stood between the people and the great god Brahma, and so were called Brahmans. It was a part of their duty to memorize the Vedas and teach them to the youth.

ful men of their caste. They perfected the Sanscrit language and used it in writing. The common people used a dialect, Prakrit. This made another barrier between learning and the people.

Rajputs. — The warrior caste is called the Rajput. It probably grew up out of the custom of rewarding the strongest and bravest soldiers with presents of lands and slaves. This is the royal stock. The name means prince, son of a rajah or king.

Vaisyas. — The third caste in descending order, made up of the agriculturists, traders, and higher craftsmen, was called Vaisya, the old name for the whole people.

These three classes were all of Aryan stock; twice-born, they called themselves.

Sudras. — The conquered non-Aryans composed the fourth or Sudra class. The Sudras were the slaves of the other castes.

THE SCYTHIANS. — About the time the Romans were making incursions into England, 100 B. C. to 500 A. D., the Rajputs of India were trying to repel the Scythians, the first of the Tartar tribes to overrun India. These Tartars, or Huns, neither conquered nor were conquered; they were absorbed, and eventually accepted the religion. The Scythians were the last of the invading people that embraced the religions of India, Buddhism and Brahmanism.

These three peoples, the Non-Aryans, the Aryans, and the Scythians, make up the people called Hindus.

Buddhism; Brahmanism; Hinduism. — Out of the Brahman religion rose, in the fifth century B.C., Buddhism. For a time it was a formidable rival of Brahmanism, but by 900 A.D. it was almost lost in India in the parent stream, though it is still the religion of millions of the people of Asia.

Buddhism. — Gautama was the son of a king of a province north of Benares. His father wished him to be a warrior like himself, but while young he renounced the world, was taught by two Brahman hermits, gave himself up to fasting and penance, and came out, after many temptations, purified, Buddha, — the Enlightened.

He began near Benares preaching, not to the sacred caste alone, as was the custom of the Brahmans, but to the common people. He converted disciples and sent them forth to spread the religion. His creed did not admit the efficacy of sacrifices or the value of the mediation of the Brahmans between God and man. He taught that "misery or happiness in this life is the unavoidable result of our conduct in a past life; and our actions here will determine our happiness or misery in the life to come." Instead of Brahman sacrifices he urged three great duties: control over self, kindness to other men, and reverence for the life of all living things. Arnold's *Light of Asia* has made the world familiar with the beautiful part of this religion. The teachings of Buddha did much to unite the people and break down caste, for Buddha's disciples taught all classes. The Brahmans taught those of the Brahman caste only. But Buddhism in India was overpowered by Brahmanism, or Hinduism, before it had completed its work.

Brahmanism. — Brahmanism took in Buddhism and other Indian beliefs, and became in time so modified that it now appears as the religious factor in Hinduism. The words Brahmanism and Hinduism seem to be used interchangeably.

Hinduism. — This is a fusion of the laws and customs of all the Hindus, and of the religions of the Aborigines, the Brahmans, and the Buddhists. Every Hindu is soaked in Hinduism. It directs his social, his business, and his religious life. It governs social and business relations by acknowledging castes, not the original four alone, but all the classes and trade guilds that have grown out of these four.

To the Oriental mind the Hindu religion is alluring, mystical, enthralling. To the Western mind it is more likely to appear merely perplexing and elusive. In order that we may understand some of the problems set for the early English rulers in India, Hinduism must be touched upon. A French traveller, André Chevrillon, who visited the cities of India and was

impressed by the philosophy of Hinduism and the
fact that it permeates all things in Benares and other
Hindu cities, says of Hinduism: [1]"We must conceive,
then, in the beginning and at the root of all things the
absolute Being, pure and void, which is at the bottom
of all forms and all germs. Developing itself outward it is subjected to Maya, illusion. . . . Illusion
being recognized as such, what is more natural than
a wish to escape from it? And how succeed in doing
this, unless by destroying in one's self all that makes
part of this illusive and fugitive world; namely, desire,
will, sensation? . . . For to immobility all Hindu
philosophy practically leads. . . . That a man may
enter into calm, he must hold his breath, fix his attention, destroy his senses, cease from speaking. He
presses his palate with the tip of his tongue, breathes
slowly, looks fixedly at a point in space, and thought
ceases, consciousness is abolished, the feeling of per-
sonality vanishes. 'We shall cease to feel pleasure
and pain, having attained immobility and solitude.' . .
'As a spider rising by means of its own thread gains
the open space, so he who meditates rises by means
of the syllable OM, and gains independence.'" This
syllable OM recalls to the Brahman the three persons
of the Hindu trinity: Brahma, the creator; Vishnu,
the preserver; Siva, the destroyer and reproducer.

[1] *In India*, André Chevrillon.

"Thought and will being abolished, the whole phantasmagoria of Maya disappears: 'We become like a fire without smoke, or like a traveller, who, having left the carriage which brought him, watches the revolution of its wheels.' . . . 'The man who sees a difference between Brahma and the world goes *from change to change, from death to death.*' That is to say, *he will forever be reborn.* . . . 'He who, knowing the Vedas and having repeated them daily in a consecrated place, having made no creature suffer, concentrates his thoughts upon the Existence, and is absorbed therein, attains the world of Brahma and returns no more; *no, he returns no more.*' . . . Such is the supreme felicity reserved for the adepts of the mysterious doctrine celebrated by the Upanishads with a solemnity of language which gives an idea of the fervor, the enthusiasm, the restrained hope wherewith the Brahman is thrilled, as he looks forward to that day of deliverance after which he will never again say *Me* of himself."

If the Hindu is striving daily to lose all sense of the *Me*, is it not possible for us to understand that he might submit with apathy to what would appear to us to be misfortune or disgrace, and even accept death with calmness and fortitude as did the Brahman Nuncomar, because he could hope to be absorbed into Brahma? Yet he might revolt in desperation against a thing that to us seems trivial, such as the greased cartridges that precipitated the Sepoy Mutiny of 1857, because he feared the pollution which would compel him to be reborn.

By the year 1000 A.D., the inhabitants of India were so imbued with Hinduism that though the different tribes were not at peace with each other, they were ready to unite and fight with a heroic determination against the invasion of people of another faith. By this time, too, the Rajputs, or soldier caste, had grown very strong and powerful, and the Vaisyas had made riches for the country.

The Mohammedans. — Meanwhile in Arabia in the seventh century Mohammedanism had sprung up. This is the religion of the Moslems. Its adherents call it Al Islam. It rests on four pillars: (1) the Koran, (2) the traditions, (3) the consent of the learned doctors, (4) the reasoning of learned divines. It enjoins five great religious duties: (1) bearing witness that there is no god but God, and Mohammed is his apostle, (2) reciting in daily prayer, (3) giving the legal alms, (4) observing the monthly feast, (5) making a pilgrimage once in a lifetime to Mecca. The followers of this new religion set out to convert the world. One of the first expeditions was against India, but the Hindus repulsed them with such valor that they got no farther than the western part of the Sind, and their foothold there they soon lost. The Mohammedan Arabs had overrun Northern Africa and conquered and settled in Spain before any incursions into India succeeded.

The following table gives the chief Mohammedan dynasties of India.

    I. House of Ghizni. 1001–1180. (Turkish.)

   II. House of Ghor. (Afghan.)

  III. The Slave Kings. (Chiefly Turkish.)

  IV. House of Khilji.

   V. House of Tughlak. 1320–1414.

      Irruption of the Moguls under Tamer (Tamerlane).

  VI. The Sayyids. 1414–1450.

 VII. The Lodis. 1450–1526. (Afghan.) Feeble reigns ; independent states multiply.

VIII. House of Tamer. (Mogul.)

      1526–1530. Baber.

      1556–1605. Akbar the Great.

      1605. Jahangir.

      1628. Shah Jahan.

      1658–1707. Aurungzebe.

      1707–1712. Bahadur Shah, or Shah Alam I.

      1748–1754. Death of Mohammed Shah, and accession of Ahmed Shah, deposed 1754.

      1754. Alamgir II. Six invasions of India by Ahmen Shah Durani, the Afghan.

      1759. Shah Alam II., titular Emperor.

      1806. Akbar, titular Emperor.

      1837–1857. Mohammed Bahadur Shah, titular Emperor ; seventeenth and last Mogul Emperor ; gave his sanction to the Mutiny of 1857, and died a state prisoner at Rangoon in 1862.

The first successful Mohammedan invasion of India founded the house of Ghizni. It was brought on by the Hindus themselves. The Hindu chief of Lahore had been annoyed by raids from the Mohammedans of Ghizni. He marched his Rajputs northwest to this town. They were repulsed; their retreat was cut off, and they barely saved themselves by promising great ransoms. When they got back to Lahore they repudiated their promises. Tradition tells that Jaipal was counselled by the Brahmans at his right hand not to disgrace himself by paying ransom to a barbarian, while his warriors on his left implored him to keep faith. The Mohammedans repaid this treachery by taking possession of Peshawar, which gave them control of both ends of the Khaibar pass. Using this pass as their gateway the Mohammedans invaded India.

The Mohammedan houses or dynasties, some Turks, some Slaves, and some Afghans, all Tartars that had become Mohammedans, fought in turn for control of Mohammedan India. The Hindu kings were defeated and routed again and again, but not subdued. Occasionally the Gurkhas and the Hillmen assisted by pouring down upon the Mohammedans, massacring thousands of them. If the Rajput kings had kept their forces together, they might have continued to withstand the Mohammedan invaders, but they quarrelled, and thus the Hindus lost control.

It was during the Slave Dynasty that the Caliph of Bagdad acknowledged India as a separate Mohammedan kingdom, and coins were struck in recognition of the new empire of Delhi in 1229.

Tughlaks. — The Tughlak dynasty was a time of oppression, and many of the Mohammedan provinces in the east and south revolted and set up independent kingdoms.

Tamer (Tamerlane). — Tamer, the Lame, described as a Mongol (Mogul) because he revived the Tartar Empire and claimed to be the representative of the great Mongol Ghenzi, Khan of the Mongols and Tartars who had conquered Pekin and northern China, made a conquering raid across India. He left no traces of his power except "days of massacre."

Petty Mohammedan Governors. — Under the weak dynasties of the Sayyids and the Lodis the petty kingdoms increased. Five independent Mohammedan states were formed in the Deccan; and the Lower Bengal district, the province of Gujarat in western India, Malwa, and the territory around Benares, each set up a separate Mohammedan government.

The Mogul Dynasty. — In the middle of the sixteenth century, the Mongols returned, this time to stay. These Mongol Tartars had been converted to Mohammedanism. Their religion was the same as that of the invaders of the Afghan and Turkish dynasties;

they differed merely in belonging to another Tartar branch and in coming in such numbers that they grew to be the great Moslem power of India. Baber, the first Great Mogul, was a descendant of Tamer, but he was a statesman as well as a warrior.

Akbar the Great. —Akbar, grandson of Baber, was the real founder of the great Mogul Empire. His dates, 1556–1605, almost coincide with those of the great English sovereign, Queen Elizabeth, 1558–1603. He showed great wisdom. He made overtures to the brave Rajputs, marrying a member of this the royal stock of the Hindus. He chose many of his generals and statesmen from the Hindus. By conquering some and conciliating others he had succeeded before his death in reducing the independent Mohammedan states to provinces of the Delhi Empire, and in bringing the Hindu kings with their subjects into political dependence upon his authority. He found India a collection of petty Hindu and Mohammedan states; he made it almost a united empire. The noble red stone fort at Agra remains to illustrate his idea of architecture. Tennyson in *Akbar's Dream* treats of the deistic religion that Akbar believed in.

Jahangir. — His son Jahangir is renowned for having as his empress "The Light of the World," and he himself is immortalized in *Lalla Rookh.* Sir Thomas Roe, the first English envoy sent out by King James in 1616, bowed low before this "the Mightie Emperour, the Great Mogul."

Shah Jahan. — This grandson of Akbar, who was contemporary with Charles I. and Cromwell of England, sat upon the great Peacock throne, now in Teheran, built the exquisite mausoleum Taj Mahal at Agra, and removed the seat of government from Agra to Delhi, where he built the Great Mosque.

Aurungzebe. — The son of Shah Jahan, Aurungzebe, added to the extent, wealth, and power of his father's possession; but it was in this reign that the decadence of the Mogul Empire began. Aurungzebe was a Mohammedan of the sternest type. He did not conciliate. He was determined to subdue the remaining independent Mohammedan powers. He succeeded, but he had only weakened Mohammedan forces that might have assisted him against the three great Hindu confederacies that had been forming — the Mahrattas, the Sikhs, and the natives of Rajputana.

A digression from the main narrative of the Moguls seems called for in order to describe the great Hindu confederacies that were the chief agents in breaking the Moslem power.

Rajputs ; Mahrattas ; Sikhs: *Rajputana.* — Aurungzebe's son deserted him and united with the Rajputs. From this time the district of Rajputana owned no allegiance to the Delhi government.

Mahrattas. — Savajee, a Hindu of South India, formed from the Hindus of the Deccan a national party called the Mahrattas from the district in which they lived. Mahratta means great country. As this army was recruited from the peasant proprietors of the land it could be quickly brought together and quickly disbanded. Savajee used his Mahrattas sometimes against the invading Mogul army of Aurungzebe, sometimes against the two independent Mohammedan states that were trying to resist Aurungzebe. His army grew powerful, and he amassed such riches that before his death he weighed himself against gold and distributed the gold to his Brahmans. He assumed the title of Rajah, king. He died in 1680. His successors were weak; the office and the power of the Mahratta kings passed from them to their Peshwas, or prime ministers. The Peshwas made Poona in Bombay the seat of government and centre of operations for the Mahrattas. They captured some provinces and compelled the Mogul Emperor to cede others to them, so that when Clive went to India this great Hindu Confederacy possessed Malwa, Nagpur, Orissa, the Lower Bengal, and the west portion of the Nizam of Hyderabad's province. By Hastings' time the Mahrattas had quarrelled among themselves and were divided into five houses. The Peshwa, with his capital at Poona, was still the nominal head. The other houses were the Bhonslas at Nagpur, the Sindhias at Gwalior, Holkar at Indore, and the Gaekwar at Baroda.

First Mahratta War, 1779–1781. — The first of the three Mahratta wars with the British is the one referred to in the *Warren Hastings* essay. It was brought on by a dispute between rivals for the Peshwa title. The French sided with one of the claimants, so the English governor at Bombay made a treaty at Surat with the other claimant to support him in return for the cession of two provinces. Hastings disapproved of the treaty, but when war began he sent troops that conquered Gujarat and Gwalior. The war closed by a treaty.

Last Mahratta War, 1817–1818. — The Mahratta dynasties, each on its own account, took up arms against the British again, and all were defeated. This broke the Mahratta power. The Gaekwar of Baroda still reigns, but his is a feudatory state only; and he spends his summers in London. Such is the fall of the Indian prince. The adopted son of the last Peshwa of Poona was the Nana Sahib of the Mutiny of 1857 fame, or infamy.

The Sikhs. — The Sikhs, a religious and military sect of the Hindus, located in the western part of the Punjab, were so cruelly persecuted by the Mohammedans that they became fanatics. They revere the

Brahmans, and forbid the slaughter of cows, but they have so few other things in common with the Hindus that they have their own national character. Every man is pledged to become a soldier, and it is said that every Sikh to this day wears a piece of steel as a sign thereof. Theirs was the last Hindu power to succumb to the English. There were two British-Sikh wars; but in 1849 the whole of the Punjab became a British province by conquest and cessions. The Punjab was laid out with roads and canals, and grew so prosperous that in the Mutiny of 1857 the Sikhs were loyal to the English.

The Moguls after Aurungzebe. — The history of the Hindu forces responsible for the breaking up of the Mogul Empire has been carried through to the time when they were merged into the Indian Empire. The account of the line of the Moguls will now be resumed. As has been said, the dissolution of the great Mogul Empire began while Aurungzebe was on the throne. Internal enemies might have completed the downfall in time, but it was not left to them alone. Persians and Afghans made raids into northern and western India, mutilating, burning, and killing as they went. The Moguls that followed Aurungzebe were weak and much harassed. In 1743 the Mogul ceded Malwa, and in 1751 Orissa to the Mahrattas, and promised an imperial grant from Bengal to the same Hindu power. The

Nizam, or Governor, of Deccan separated the Deccan from the Delhi Empire; and the Vizier, or Prime Minister, of Oude set up a separate dynasty and took for himself the title of Nabob Vizier of Oude.

In 1764 the Nabob Vizier of Oude and the Great Mogul, Shah Alam II., combined against the English. They were defeated at the battle of Baxar. The Mogul became a pensioner of the English, and from that time the Moguls were only titular. In exchange for her protection, the Mogul ceded Great Britain the provinces of Bengal, Orissa, and Bahar, and the following year the northern Circars. The English allotted Corah and Allahabad to the Mogul, and he held his court at Allahabad.

In 1771 Shah Alam determined to try to regain the throne at Delhi. The Mahrattas were the only strong power aside from the English, so he attached himself to them. They seated him at Delhi, but then immediately compelled him and his army to assist them in a marauding raid on the Rohillas. He became disgusted with the faithlessness of the Mahrattas and tried to withdraw from them, but they would not allow him to, and compelled him to be an instrument in their hands. One of his acts at this time was to cede Allahabad and Corah to the Mahrattas; but the English took possession of them. The English debated their responsibility toward the unhappy Mogul in his captivity, but decided it would not be politic to interfere. In the second war of the Mahrattas and English in 1803 Delhi was taken, and the poor, blind, old Emperor Shah Alam passed once more under English protection.

The last of the Great Moguls, Mohammed Bahadur Shah, was living in Delhi on English bounty when the Great Mutiny of 1857 broke out. The mutineers proclaimed him the Great Emperor. When the English recovered the city, he was captured and was imprisoned for life. The princes were shot.

THE BRITISH IN INDIA

In the fifteenth century the powers of Europe were trying to find a new route to India. Columbus sailed west carrying a letter to the Khan of Tartary, and discovered America instead of the new route; but Vasco da Gama rounded the Cape of Good Hope in 1498 and landed on the west coast of India. Thus Portugal was the first Christian country to get a foothold in India. The Portuguese established trading-posts at Surat and Goa on the west coast. They were followed by the Dutch, who established their posts on the islands along the east coast. Both nations had secured a good trade with India before the English ventures began. The Dutch traders were growing rich from the pepper and other products of India. This incited the English merchants, now that the way was open, to form a company to trade in the East Indies.

An association was formed with 125 shareholders, merchants of London, and a capital stock of £70,000. This was the organization of the famous English East India Company, and it received the royal charter from Queen Elizabeth on the last day of the year 1600.

For years there were sea fights for the right to trade with the islands and along the coast of India. In the first years of the seventeenth century the Portuguese were driven from all the west coast, except Goa, and the English East India Company established factories. The Dutch drove the English from the islands on the east coast, but this resulted in English settlements on the peninsula itself. The early traders seem to have stood in awe of the Great Mogul, believing the native population to be one people united under one emperor; but when the English were driven from the Archipelago, they gradually procured licenses from the Great Mogul to establish factories on the mainland. In 1639 the site of the present city of Madras was purchased by the East India Company from the Rajah of Chandrigiri, and Fort St. George was built. This was the first territory owned by the Company. The island of Bombay was ceded by Portugal to the British Crown, and in 1668 King Charles II. sold his rights over Bombay to the East India Company. The Company had more difficulty in getting a settlement in the province of Bengal. It was not until 1700 that they were able to purchase three Indian villages there, that were on the site of the present city of Calcutta. In this way the three great presidencies, Madras, Bombay, and Calcutta, had their beginnings.

Until the end of the seventeenth century the English had thought of trading only. But uprisings of the Mahrattas against the Moguls taught the English that the Great Mogul was not the undisputed ruler of India.

Petty wars with both Mahrattas and Moguls showed
the English that they would be compelled to acquire territory in order to protect their trade. The three great
centres had been established, Bombay, Madras, and
Calcutta; and the Company, about 1685, sent out Sir
John Child with power to make war or peace and
arrange for the safety of the Company. His title was
Governor-General, a title that died with him and was
not revived until it was given to Warren Hastings.
The financial success of the East India Company was
continuous. This caused rivalry and the formation of
other English East India companies, but in every case
the "interloper," whether a company or an individual,
was taken into the original association, so that from
1600 to 1858 the name English East India Company
stands for one organization. During the seventeenth century the French organized a French East India Company
similar to the Dutch and English companies. The
French and English traded side by side without the
rivalry that had existed between the English and the
other European nations, until the war of the Austrian
succession made the representatives of France and
England in India fear each other. During the difficulties that arose at this time the French captured
Madras, and although it was restored to the English
by the terms of the treaty entered into by the home
government at Aix-la-Chapelle, the French success

influenced the native rulers later to side with the French and feel contempt for the English. The French were more diplomatic than the English and more affable to the native chiefs, and so had gained many favors from the Emperor at Delhi, the Great Mogul, such as being allowed to coin money for the provinces of the Carnatic. By the middle of the eighteenth century the French had a lucrative trade in India, with posts at Pondicherry in the Carnatic and Chandernagor near Calcutta.

Dupleix in 1741 was made Governor of Pondicherry with supreme control over French India. Southern India, after the death of the Great Mogul Aurungzebe, had divided up into states that declared themselves independent of the Mogul. By supporting the claims of two native chiefs, one for the Carnatic and one for the Deccan, Dupleix became a political power. In self-defence the English espoused the cause of a rival chief for the Carnatic, Mohammed Ali, afterward known as the "Nabob of Arcot." It was at this time that Clive, a young man of twenty-four, without military training, came forward with a plan to recover lost ground for the English. He was listened to and allowed troops. The account of the struggle between the French and the English for the control of the Carnatic, and the success of the English; and the further account of Clive's successes in Bengal, where he conquered the army of Surajah Dowlah, revenged the tragedy of the Black Hole, fought the battle of Plassey, made Meer Jaffier Nabob of Bengal, and silenced the French and Dutch forever in the "Garden of India," — the account of all this is vividly given in Macaulay's *Lord Clive*. It was in the events following the battle of Plassey that Warren Hastings' active life began, and there begins Macaulay's account of him. As has been said, the object of the East India Company at first had been trade merely. The opposition of the Portuguese, Dutch, and French, and the unsettled condition of the native rulers, forced the first fights upon them to protect their property ; in time this seemed to demand that they should become the aggressors, and when Hastings went to India the battle of Plassey had settled the policy of England in India as one of conquest.

The *Warren Hastings* essay continues the account of the British in India from Clive's time to 1785. The remainder of this article will describe briefly the events from 1785 to the time of settled government.

After Hastings left India there was a revolt of the Sikhs, but the English conquered them and the Punjab was annexed as English territory. This with lesser victories seemed to give all India to the control of the English Company, and it had never seemed so strong nor so secure in its monopoly. In 1857 the native element of the army, by being recruited to assist against the Mahrattas, Afghans, and Sikhs, had grown to about 350,000 men, while the European part numbered only about 25,000. With these figures before us we can understand the great Sepoy Mutiny. The *Rulers of India* series gives a full account of the Mutiny, and Mrs. Steele in her novel *On the Face of the Waters* has made the capture of Delhi by the Sepoys, the siege of Lucknow, and the surrender and massacre at Cawnpore, seem horribly real. The Mutiny was put down, but it had brought home to English statesmen the need of formal acceptance of the responsibilities of government in India. In the spring of 1858 the Mutiny was broken; in the fall of that year the East India Company's rule terminated, and the sovereignty of the Queen was declared.

For two hundred and fifty-eight years the East India Company controlled and directed the political and military government of India. They went to India as traders; to protect their interests they became conquerors and administrators. They made India a possession of Great Britain, and for years were in the curious position of a company of merchants vested with the control of a whole empire. It was not until 1858 that England took the entire administration of the government of India into her own hands.

A Summary of the chief Acts of Parliament relating to the East India Company

1600. The original charter was granted by Queen Elizabeth. It gave to the Company the exclusive privilege of the India trade.

1773. The Regulating Act was passed, whose chief provisions are given in the *Warren Hastings* essay.

1784. Pitt's India Bill passed. This founded the Board of Control in England. This Board was authorized to superintend, direct, and control all acts, operations, and concerns relating to the civil and military government of India. It was empowered to send out troops to India at the expense of the Company. The Directors of the Company were required to submit all papers to this Board except those relating to commercial matters. The phrase Governor-General-in-Council originated at this time.

1813. Parliament renewed the charter for twenty years, but abolished the Company's monopoly of Indian trade. The appointment of governor-general, governor, and commander-in-chief was no longer valid without the consent of the crown.

1833. The charter was renewed for another twenty
years. It put an end to the Company's
exclusive right to the China trade. Reforms
were introduced in the constitution for Indian government. A new legal member, not
necessarily a servant of the Company, was
added to the Board of Control. Macaulay
was the first man sent to India in this
capacity. A Law Commission was appointed.
The Governor-General-in-Council was given
control over all the Presidencies, in civil
and military administration.

1853. The charter was renewed for an indefinite time.

1858. The Act for the Better Government of India
passed. It transferred the administration
from the Company to the crown.

The Present Government of India

In 1876 Queen Victoria assumed the title of Empress of India. India is now divided into British and
Feudatory India. British India is divided into twelve
Provinces. Each has its own governor, but all are
under the supreme control of the Governor-General-
in-Council, who bears the title, also, of Viceroy of
India. The Viceroy and the governors of Madras

and Bombay are appointed by the Queen. The governors of the other provinces are nominated by the Viceroy, from the Anglo-Indian service. Calcutta is the seat of government in the winter, and Simla in the Himalayas in the summer. There are Legislative Councils in the various provinces, and in 1893 the first general election to the Legislative Councils was held.

Feudatory India consists of states governed by native princes, under the advice of a British Resident stationed at each court by the Viceroy. Some of these princes have more power than others, but all are limited by treaties in which they acknowledge the suzerainty of the British Government. The feudatory states are not allowed to make war on each other, or to make alliances with foreign powers. Questions of intervention of outside powers in India are now treated the same as encroachments on any other soil belonging to the Queen's Government.

INDIAN TERMS

The Indian Government has adopted a system of pronunciation for the words in common use. The vowels are sounded as in Latin. The accents marked on the words below are authorized. The best authorities differ in their spelling, so two or three are given. Macaulay's is put first, though usually it is not the most common.

Great Mogul', Mughal. Mogul, the name of the last Mohammedan Dynasty that ruled in India. Great Mogul, title of the emperor of the Moguls, who claimed to be emperor of all India.

Na'bob, Nawab. Mohammedan title for the ruler of a province, equivalent to governor or viceroy. Nabob of Bengal.

Vizier', Vazir, Vizir. Mohammedan title for a state minister, or prime minister. Nabob Vizier of Oude, governor and prime minister of Oude.

Shah. Persian title equivalent to king. Padisha, king of kings, a title sometimes taken by the Great Mogul. Shah Alam, the last of the Great Moguls.

Nizam. Hindu title equivalent to regulator, governor. Nizam of Hyderabad. It often carried the idea of regulator of political and judicial affairs.

Be'gum. Hindu title for princess. Munny Begum, mother princess.

Diwan', Dewan. A head officer of finance.

Dow'lah. Mohammedan title equivalent to governor. *ow* as *ou* in *out*. Sura'jah Dowlah, one of the Nabobs of Bengal.

Ra'jah, Raja. Hindu title for king. Rajah of Benares.

Rajput', Rajpoot. Name of Hindu caste from which the king
    was chosen. It means son of a king, prince.

Rajputa'na. Name of a district occupied by a strong tribe of
    the Rajputs.

Punjab', Panjab. Name of a district occupied by the Hindus.
    The Sikhs were in the Punjab.

Khan. Persian title for king or prince; but like all these titles
    it often meant nothing more than an assumed distinction,
    as our esquire.

Pesh'wa. A title meaning prime minister. Among the Mah-
    rattas the prime minister usurped the rights of the king,
    so peshwa came to mean ruler. Peshwa of Poona, ruler
    of the Mahrattas, with his capital at Poona.

Nuncomar', Savajee', Cheyt'e Sing (Chāt Sing).

Aurungzebe' (Awrungzāb), *Hy'der A'li.*

Dec'can. It means the south. A name given to the southern
    part of the peninsula of India.

Oude, Oudh. A province. *ou* as in *out. e* is silent.

Hima'laya. Snow-abode, the word means.

MACAULAY'S WORKS

Essays Published in Knight's Quarterly Magazine.
    Fragments of a Roman Tale, 1823.
    On the Royal Society of Literature, 1823.
    Scenes from Athenian Revels, 1824.
    Criticisms on the Principal Italian Writers, No. 1
        Dante, No. 2 Petrarch, 1824.
    **Some account of the Great Lawsuit between the Par-
    ishes of St. Denis and St. George in the Water, 1824.**

A Conversation of Mr. Abraham Cowley and Mr. John
Milton touching the Great Civil War, 1824.

On the Athenian Orators, 1824.

A Prophetic Account of a Grand National Epic, to be
entitled "The Wellingtoniad," and to be published
in 2824, 1824.

On Mitford's History of Greece, 1824.

Essays Published in EDINBURGH REVIEW.

The West Indies, Jan., 1825.

Milton, August, 1825.

The London University, Jan., 1826.

Social and Industrial Capacities of Negroes, March,
1827.

Machiavelli, March, 1827.

The Present Administration, June, 1827.

John Dryden, Jan., 1828.

History, May, 1828.

Hallam's Constitutional History, Sept., 1828.

Mill on Government, March, 1829.

Westminster Reviewer's Defence of Mill, June, 1829.

Utilitarian Theory of Government, Oct., 1829.

Southey's Colloquies on Society, Jan., 1830.

Mr. Robert Montgomery's Poems, April, 1830.

Sadler's Law of Population, July, 1830.

Southey's Edition of the Pilgrim's Progress, Dec., 1830.

Sadler's Refutation Refuted, Jan., 1831.

Civil Disabilities of the Jews, Jan., 1831.

Moore's Life of Lord Byron, June, 1831.

Croker's Edition of Boswell's Life of Johnson, Sept.,
1831.

Lord Nugent's Memorial of Hampden, Dec., 1831.

Burleigh and His Times, April, 1832.

Edinburgh Election, May, 1839.

Confidence in the Ministry of Lord Melbourne, Jan., 1840.

War with China, April, 1840.

Copyright, Feb., 1841.

Copyright, April, 1842.

The People's Charter, May, 1842.

The Gates of Somnauth, March, 1842.

The Treaty of Washington, March, 1843.

The State of Ireland, Feb. 1844.

Dissenters' Chapels Bill, June, 1844.

Post Office Espionage, July, 1844.

Opening Letters in the Post Office, July, 1844.

The Sugar Duties, Feb., 1845.

Maynooth, April, 1845.

The Church of Ireland, April, 1845.

Theological Tests of the Scotch Universities, July, 1845.

Corn Laws, Dec., 1845.

The Ten Hour Bill, May, 1846.

The Literature of Britain, Nov., 1846.

Education, April, 1847.

Inaugural Speech at Glasgow College, March, 1849.

Re-election to Parliament, Nov., 1852.

Exclusion of Judges from the House of Commons, June, 1853.

Introductory Report upon the Indian Penal Code, Oct., 1837.

Notes on the Penal Code (140 pages of close print).

History.

The History of England —

From the Accession of James the Second.   6 vols.

Poetry.

Pompeii. This poem obtained the Chancellor's medal at Cambridge University in 1819.

Evening.   This poem obtained the Chancellor's medal in 1821.

Lays of Ancient Rome.

    Horatius.

    The Battle of Lake Regillus.

    Virginia.

    The Prophecy of Capys.

Epitaph on Henry Martyn.

Lines to the Memory of Pitt.

A Radical War Song.

Ivry.

The Battle of Moncontour.

Songs of the Civil War.

Sermon in a Churchyard.

Translations from A. V. Arnault.

Dies Irae.

The Marriage of Tirzah and Ahirad.

The Country Gentleman's Trip to Cambridge.

Song.

The Deliverance of Vienna.

The Armada.

Inscription on the Statue of Lord Bentinck.

Epitaph on Sir Benjamin Heath Malkin.

The Last Buccaneer.

Epitaph on a Jacobite.

Epitaph on Lord Metcalfe.

Translations from Plautus.

Valentine.

Paraphrase of a Passage in the Chronicle of the Monk of
    St. Gall.

Lines Written on the Night of the 30th of July, 1847.

Rosamond.

Battle of Naseby.

CONTEMPORANEOUS HISTORY

WARREN HASTINGS IN INDIA, 1750–1785

GEORGE II., 1727–1760

Frederick the Great, King of Prussia, 1740–1786.
Clive takes Arcot, 1751.
Seven Years' War with France, 1756.
French and Indian War in America, 1755–1760.
"The Black Hole" of Calcutta, 1756.
Clive wins battle of Plassey, 1757.
Victory of Quebec (England gains Canada), 1759.

GEORGE III., 1760–1820

Catherine II., Russia, 1762.
Stamp Act, 1765 (repealed 1766).
Letters of "Junius," 1769.
Conquest of Corsica, 1769.
Napoleon and Wellington born, 1769.
Debates in Parliament regularly reported, 1771.
Pressing to death abolished, 1772.
"The Boston Tea Party," 1773.
The American Revolution begins, 1775.
Free trade granted to Ireland, 1776.
Lord George Gordon riots, 1780.
Defeat of Cornwallis at Yorktown, 1781.
Treaties of Paris and Versailles, 1783.

MACAULAY, 1800–1859

ENGLISH MEN OF LETTERS

Sir Walter Scott.
  Lady of the Lake.
  Lay of the Last Minstrel.
  Ivanhoe, Waverley.
John Wilson (Christopher North).
  Noctes Ambrosianæ.
Hannah More.
  Search after Happiness.
  Practical Piety.
Frances Burney (Madame d'Arblay).
  Evelina.
George Gordon (Lord Byron).
  Childe Harold.
  Prisoner of Chillon.
Thomas Moore.
  Lalla Rookh.
Percy Bysshe Shelley.
  The Cloud.
  To the Skylark.
  To the Nightingale.
John Keats.
  Eve of St. Agnes.
William Wordsworth.
  The Excursion.
  Ode to Immortality.
Samuel T. Coleridge.
  Ancient Mariner.
  Lectures on Shakespeare.

Richard Brinsley Sheridan.
>   *The Rivals.*
>   *The School for Scandal.*

Henry Hallam.
>   *Constitutional History of England.*

Thomas Arnold (Master at Rugby).

Thomas Carlyle.
>   *The French Revolution.*
>   *Sartor Resartus.*
>   *Frederick the Great.*
>   *On the Choice of Books.*

Harriet Martineau.
>   *History of England, 1816–1846.*

William Ewart Gladstone.
>   *Studies in Homer.*

James A. Froude.
>   *Short Studies on Great Subjects.*

James Mill.
>   *History of British India.*

John Stuart Mill.
>   *System of Logic.*

John Ruskin.
>   *Lessons on Architecture and Painting.*
>   *Sesame and Lilies.*

Herbert Spencer.
>   *First Principles, Biology.*

Sir John Herschel.
>   *Outlines of Astronomy.*

Charles Darwin.
>   *Origin of Species.*

Francis Jeffrey, Reviewer.
>   *Edited the Edinburgh Review, 1802–1809.*

Charles Lamb.
> *Essays of Elia.*

Thomas De Quincey.
> *Flight of a Tartar Tribe.*
> *Confessions of an English Opium Eater.*

Matthew Arnold.
> *Critical and Political Essays.*
> *Tristram and Iseult.*

Jane Austen.
> *Sense and Sensibility.*
> *Pride and Prejudice.*

William M. Thackeray.
> *The Newcomes.*
> *Henry Esmond.*

Charles Dickens.
> *Pickwick Papers.*
> *David Copperfield.*

George Eliot.
> *Silas Marner.*
> *Mill on the Floss.*
> *Middlemarch.*
> *Romola.*

Elizabeth B. Browning.
> *A Vision of Poets.*
> *A Musical Instrument.*

Alfred Tennyson.
> *Idyls of the King.*
> *In Memoriam.*

Robert Browning.
> *Saul.*
> *Ring and the Book.*

AMERICAN MEN OF LETTERS

Daniel Webster, Statesman and Orator.
  Bunker Hill Orations.
  Reply to Hayne.
Henry Clay, Statesman and Orator.
John Calhoun, Statesman and Orator.
  Life of Washington.
  Life of Goldsmith.
Washington Irving.
  Sketch Book.
  Bracebridge Hall.
  The Alhambra.
James Fenimore Cooper.
  Red Rover.
  The Pilot.
  Last of the Mohicans.
  The Spy.
John James Audubon, Naturalist.
William Cullen Bryant.
  Little People of the Snow.
  Robert of Lincoln.
  To a Waterfowl.
Francis Scott Key.
  The Star Spangled Banner.
John Howard Payne.
  Home, Sweet Home.
Edgar Allan Poe.
  The Raven.
  The Gold Bug.
  Murders in the Rue Morgue.

Ralph Waldo Emerson, "The Sage of Concord."
  Representative Men.
  American Scholar.
  The Snow Storm.
  Wood Notes.
Louis Agassiz, Naturalist.
Henry D. Thoreau.
  A Week on the Concord and Merrimac Rivers.
  Walden, or Life in the Woods.
William Lloyd Garrison, Abolitionist.
William Hickling Prescott.
  Ferdinand and Isabella.
  Conquest of Mexico.
Horace Greeley, Editor of *New York Tribune.*
  Recollections of a Busy Life.
John Lothrop Motley.
  Rise of the Dutch Republic.
  History of the United Netherlands.
Bayard Taylor, Traveller.
  Land of the Saracens.
  Views Afoot.
Oliver Wendell Holmes.
  Autocrat of the Breakfast Table.
  The Last Leaf.
  The Chambered Nautilus.
  Over the Tea-cups.
Henry Wadsworth Longfellow.
  Evangeline.
  Song of Hiawatha.
  Translation of Dante's Divina Commedia.
John Greenleaf Whittier.
  Snow Bound.

> *Tent on the Beach.*
> *My Soul and I.*

Mrs. Julia Ward Howe.
> *Battle Hymn of the Republic.*

James Russell Lowell.
> *Among My Books.*
> *Vision of Sir Launfal.*
> *Commemoration Ode.*
> *Fable for Critics.*

Nathaniel Hawthorne.
> *House of Seven Gables.*
> *Marble Faun.*

Abraham Lincoln, Statesman.

MEN OF NOTE OF OTHER COUNTRIES

Goethe, German author.
Beethoven, German composer.
Paganini, Italian violinist.
Napoleon, military genius, Emperor of **France.**
Guizot, French historian.
Kant, German metaphysician.
Hegel, German philosopher.
Froebel, German educator.
Schopenhauer, German philosopher.
Moltke, Prussian general.
Hans Christian Andersen, Danish author.
Victor Hugo, French novelist.

BIBLIOGRAPHY

BOOKS ON MACAULAY

The Life and Letters of Lord Macaulay, 2 vols. G. Otto Trevelyan.

Macaulay. English Men of Letters Series. J. Cotter Morison.

Macaulay. Whipple's Essays and Reviews, Vol. 1.

Macaulay. Matthew Arnold's Mixed Essays.

Macaulay. Minto's Manual of English Prose Literature.

Macaulay. Gladstone's Gleanings of Past Years.

Macaulay. Bagehot's Estimate of Some Englishmen and Scotchmen.

Macaulay. McCarthy's Short History of Our Own Times.

Macaulay. Wilson's Essays, Critical and Imaginative.

Macaulay. Clark's Study of English Prose Writing.

BOOKS ON INDIA

A History of British Empire. Sir Wm. W. Hunter. A Vice-President of the Royal Asiatic Society.

A Brief History of the Indian Peoples. Sir Wm. W. Hunter. The arrangement is on a system that makes the book a clear, succinct account. If only one book on India can be bought, I should advise the purchase of this one. Oxford, Clarendon Press.

Epochs of Indian History Series.

    Ancient History (2000 B.C.–800 A.D.). Romesh Chunder Dutt, C. I. E.

    The Muhammadans. J. D. Rees, Madras Civil Service.

    The Mahrattas. K. T. Telang, Judge of the High Court, Bombay.

History of British Empire, 10 Vols. Mill and Wilson.

Rise of the British Power in the East. Hon. Montstuart Elphinstone. A full history to the battle of Panipat, 1765.

The Story of the Empire Series.
> *The Rise of the Empire.* Sir Walter Besant.
> *The Story of India.* Demetrius C. Boulger.

How the British won India. W. Plimblett. This book is in popular reading style.

In India. André Chevrillon. (Henry Holt and Co.) A fascinating book of travels in India.

History of the Indian Mutiny. T. Rice Holmes. (Good maps.)

On the Face of the Waters. Mrs. Flora Annie Steele. A novel that tells the story of the Sepoy Mutiny of 1857. Mrs. Steele was a teacher in the Punjab for twenty years.

Sacred Books of the East. Max Müller.

Buddhism. Professor Rhys Davids.

History of the Mughal Emperors of Hindustan. Stanley Lane-Poole.

Out of India. Rudyard Kipling.

From Sea to Sea. Rudyard Kipling.

Soldiers Three. Rudyard Kipling.

Hastings and the Rohilla War. Sir John Strachey.

Story of Nuncomar and Impeachment of Sir Elijah Impey. Sir James Fitzjames Stephen.

Rulers of India Series. (Clarendon Press.)
> Lord Clive.
> Dupleix.
> Warren Hastings.
> Sir John (Lord) Lawrence.

India Revisited. Sir Edwin Arnold.

Forty-one Years in India. Frederick Sleigh Roberts.

Nabob of Arcot's Debts. Edmund Burke's Works.

Speech on Mr. Fox's East India Bill. Edmund Burke's Works.

A SUGGESTED METHOD OF STUDY

First, read rapidly the *India* and the *British in India* in the *Introduction* and glance at the map when names of places occur. Second, read the essay through as one would a story, simply for the story; afterward, it may be studied as a biography and an essay.

Macaulay has allowed the periods of Hastings' life to govern the divisions of the essay. These parts are readily seen on a second reading; and form the main sections into which the outline falls. Take up the first paragraphs and examine them to see whether they belong under the first division or go to form an introduction to the whole essay. As the introduction and the conclusion are considered the most difficult parts of writing to the young essayist it may be well to notice how simply and naturally Macaulay begins and ends his essays.

After the introduction is examined, each part may be taken up as a unit. Find what the author proposed to tell in each division and discuss his method of telling it by settling definitely the function of each paragraph in carrying on the story.

While studying the purpose of the author, his style of expression may be studied also; but the more natural and interesting method seems to be to study the whole essay, division by division, to get reform. The Directors notified to him their high approbation, and were so much pleased with his conduct that they determined to place him at the head of the government of Bengal. Early in 1772 he quitted Fort St. George for his new post. The Imhoffs, who 5 were still man and wife, accompanied him, and lived at Calcutta on the same plan which they had already followed during more than two years.

When Hastings took his seat at the head of the council board, Bengal was still governed according to 10 the system which Clive had devised, a system which was, perhaps, skilfully contrived for the purpose of facilitating and concealing a great revolution, but which, when that revolution was complete and irrevocable, could produce nothing but inconvenience. 15 There were two governments, the real and the ostensible. The supreme power belonged to the Company, and was in truth the most despotic power that can be conceived. The only restraint on the English masters of the country was that which their own justice and 20 humanity imposed on them. There was no constitutional check on their will, and resistance to them was utterly hopeless.

But, though thus absolute in reality, the English had not yet assumed the style of sovereignty. They 25

held their territories as vassals of the °throne of Delhi;
they raised their revenues as collectors appointed by
the imperial commission: their public seal was inscribed with the imperial titles; and their mint struck
5 only the imperial coin.

There was still a nabob of Bengal, who stood to the
English rulers of his country in the same relation in
which °Augustulus stood to Odoacer, or the last °Mero-
vingians to Charles Martel and Pepin. He lived at
10 Moorshedabad, surrounded by princely magnificence.
He was approached with outward marks of reverence,
and his name was used in public instruments. But
in the government of the country he had less real
share than the youngest writer or cadet in the Com-
15 pany's service.

The English council which represented the Company
at Calcutta was constituted on a very different plan
from that which has since been adopted. At present
the °Governor is, as to all executive measures, abso-
20 lute. He can declare war, conclude peace, appoint
public functionaries or remove them, in opposition to
the unanimous sense of those who sit with him in
council. They are, indeed, entitled to know all that
is done, to discuss all that is done, to advise, to re-
25 monstrate, to send protests to England. But it is with

the Governor that the supreme power resides, and on
him that the whole responsibility rests. This system,
which was introduced by Mr. Pitt and Mr. Dundas in
spite of the strenuous opposition of Mr. Burke, we
conceive to be on the whole the best that was ever 5
devised for the government of a country where no
materials can be found for a representative constitution. In the time of Hastings the Governor had only
one vote in council, and, in case of an equal division,
a casting vote. It therefore happened not unfre- 10
quently that he was overruled on the gravest questions; and it was possible that he might be wholly
excluded, for years together, from the real direction of
public affairs.

The English functionaries at Fort William had as 15
yet paid little or no attention to the internal government of Bengal. The only branch of politics about
which they much busied themselves was negotiation
with the native princes. The police, the administration of justice, the details of the collection of revenue, 20
were almost entirely neglected. We may remark that
the phraseology of the Company's servants still bears
the traces of this state of things. To this day they
always use the word "political" as synonymous with
"diplomatic." We could name a gentleman still liv- 25

ing, who was described by the highest authority as an
invaluable public servant, eminently fit to be at the
head of the internal administration of a whole presidency, but unfortunately quite ignorant of all politi-
5 cal business.

The internal government of Bengal the English
rulers delegated to a great native minister, who was
stationed at Moorshedabad. All military affairs, and,
with the exception of what pertains to mere ceremo-
10 nial, all foreign affairs, were withdrawn from his control; but the other departments of the administration
were entirely confided to him. His own stipend
amounted to near a hundred thousand pounds sterling a year. The personal allowance of the nabob,
15 amounting to more than three hundred thousand
pounds a year, passed through the minister's hands,
and was, to a great extent, at his disposal. The collection of the revenue, the administration of justice,
the maintenance of order, were left to this high func-
20 tionary; and for the exercise of his immense power
he was responsible to none but the British masters of
the country.

A situation so °important, lucrative, and splendid,
was naturally an object of ambition to the ablest and
25 most powerful natives. Clive had found it difficult to

at the author's mind, then to return for comment on the devices he used in presenting his subject. It is impossible to read the essay twice without noticing his wealth of words and his exact use of them; and without recognizing the value of his figures, allusions, balanced structures, climaxes, repetitions, and the many other arts used to make his meaning clear and his work inviting. So the passages best adapted to intensive study will be forechosen.

Those who have written on Macaulay's style have given to us a variety of verdicts. Critics say of his style that it is pointed, epigrammatic, rapid, clear, harsh, vigorous, animated, simple, concrete, picturesque. They say he is fond of balanced structure, repetition, climax, the short sentence, enumeration of particulars, antithesis; that he has great erudition, splendor of imagery, the power of selection that seizes upon what is striking, the art of persuasion, taste, melody, harmony, pathos. They say of him, too, that he is a master of the mechanical art of putting words together; that is, of clear sentence structure and logical paragraph building. Trying to prove or disprove the justness of these various estimates is an interesting and profitable way to form one's own opinion.

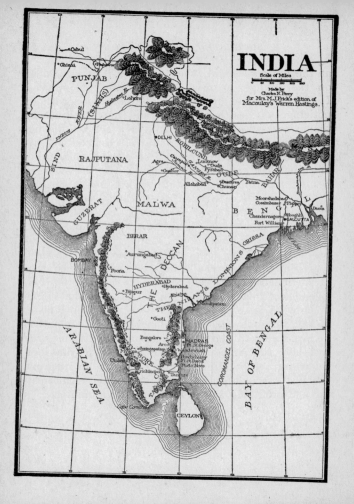

INDIA

Scale of Miles

Made by
Charles N. Perry
for Mrs. M. J. Frick's edition of
Macaulay's Warren Hastings.

WARREN HASTINGS

(1841)

Memoirs of the Life of Warren Hastings, First Governor-General of Bengal. Compiled from Original Papers, by the Rev. G. R. GLEIG, M.A. 3 vols. 8vo. London: 1841.

WE are inclined to think that we shall best meet the wishes of our readers, if, instead of minutely examining this book, we attempt to give, in a way necessarily hasty and imperfect, our own view of the life and character of Mr. Hastings. Our feeling towards him is not 5 exactly that of the House of Commons which impeached him in 1787; neither is it that of the House of Commons which °uncovered and stood up to receive him in 1813. He had great qualities, and he rendered great services to the state. But to represent him as a man 10 of stainless virtue is to make him ridiculous; and from a regard for his memory, if from no other feeling, his friends would have done well to lend no countenance to such adulation. We believe that, if he were now living, he would have sufficient judgment and sufficient 15 greatness of mind to wish to be shown as he was. He

B   1

must have known that there were dark spots on his fame. He might also have felt with pride that the splendor of his fame would bear many spots. He would have wished posterity to have a likeness of him, though an unfavorable likeness, rather than a daub at once insipid and unnatural, resembling neither him nor any body else. "Paint me as I am," said Oliver Cromwell, while sitting to young Lely. "If you leave out the scars and wrinkles, I will not pay you a shilling." Even in such a trifle, the great Protector showed both his good sense and his magnanimity. He did not wish all that was characteristic in his countenance to be lost, in the vain attempt to give him the regular features and smooth blooming cheeks of the curl-pated minions of James the First. He was content that his face should go forth marked with all the blemishes which had been put on it by time, by war, by sleepless nights, by anxiety, perhaps by remorse; but with valor, policy, authority, and public care written in all its princely lines. If men truly great knew their own interest, it is thus that they would wish their minds to be portrayed.

Warren Hastings sprang from an ancient and illustrious race. It has been affirmed that his pedigree can be traced back to the great Danish sea-king, whose sails were long the terror of both coasts of the Bristol Channel, and who, after many fierce and doubtful struggles, yielded at last to the valor and genius of Alfred. But the undoubted splendor of the line of Hastings needs no illustration from fable. One branch of that line wore, in the fourteenth century, the coronet of Pembroke. From another branch sprang the renowned °Chamberlain, the faithful adherent of the White Rose, whose fate has furnished so striking a theme both to poets and to historians. His family received from the Tudors the earldom of Huntingdon, which, after long dispossession, was regained in our time by a series of events scarcely paralleled in romance.

The lords of the manor of Daylesford, in Worcestershire, claimed to be considered as the heads of this distinguished family. The main stock, indeed, prospered less than some of the younger shoots. But the Daylesford family, though not ennobled, was wealthy and highly considered, till, about two hundred years ago, it was overwhelmed by the great ruin of the civil war. °The Hastings of that time was a zealous cavalier. He raised money on his lands, sent his plate to the °mint at Oxford, joined the royal army, and, after spending half his property in the cause of King Charles, was glad to ransom himself by making

over most of the remaining half to speaker Lenthal.
The old seat at Daylesford still remained in the family;
but it could no longer be kept up; and in the following
generation it was sold to a merchant of London.

5 Before this transfer took place, the last Hastings of
Daylesford had presented his second son to the rectory
of the parish in which the ancient residence of the
family stood. The °living was of little value; and
the situation of the poor clergyman, after the sale
10 of the estate, was deplorable. He was constantly
engaged in lawsuits about his °tithes with the new
lord of the manor, and was at length utterly ruined.
His eldest son, Howard, a well-conducted young man,
obtained a place in the Customs. The second son,
15 Pynaston, an idle worthless boy, married before he
was sixteen, lost his wife in two years, and died in the
West Indies, leaving to the care of his unfortunate
father a little orphan, destined to strange and memorable vicissitudes of fortune.

20 Warren, the son of Pynaston, was born on the sixth
of December, 1732. His mother died a few days
later, and he was left dependent on his distressed
grandfather. The child was early sent to the village
school, where he learned his letters on the same bench
25 with the sons of the peasantry; nor did any thing in

his garb or fare indicate that his life was to take a widely different course from that of the young rustics with whom he studied and played. But no cloud could overcast the dawn of so much genius and so much ambition. The very ploughmen observed, and long remembered, how kindly little Warren took to his book. The daily sight of the lands which his ancestors had possessed, and which had passed into the hands of strangers, filled his young brain with wild fancies and projects. He loved to hear stories of the wealth and greatness of his progenitors, of their splendid housekeeping, their loyalty, and their valor. On one bright summer day, the boy, then just seven years old, lay on the bank of the rivulet which flows through the old domain of his house to join the Isis. There, as threescore and ten years later he told the tale, rose in his mind a scheme which, through all the turns of his eventful career, was never abandoned. He would recover the estate which had belonged to his fathers. He would be Hastings of Daylesford. This purpose, formed in infancy and poverty, grew stronger as his intellect expanded and as his fortune rose. He pursued his plan with that calm but indomitable force of will which was the most striking peculiarity of his character. When, under a tropical

sun, he ruled fifty millions of Asiatics, his hopes,
amidst all the cares of war, finance, and legislation,
still pointed to Daylesford.   And when his long
public life, so singularly chequered with good and
5 evil, with glory and obloquy, had at length closed for
ever, it was to Daylesford that he retired to die.

When he was eight years old, his uncle Howard
determined to take charge of him, and to give him a
liberal education.   The boy went up to London, and
10 was sent to a school at Newington, where he was well
taught but ill fed.   He always attributed the small-
ness of his stature to the hard and scanty fare of this
seminary.   At ten he was removed to Westminster
school, then flourishing under the care of Dr. Nichols.
15 Vinny Bourne, as his pupils affectionately called him,
was one of the masters.   °Churchill, Colman, Lloyd,
Cumberland, Cowper, were among the students.   With
Cowper Hastings formed a friendship which neither
the lapse of time, nor a wide dissimilarity of opinions
20 and pursuits, could wholly dissolve.   It does not
appear that they ever met after they had grown to
manhood.   But forty years later, when the voices of
many great orators were crying for vengeance on the
oppressor of India, the shy and secluded poet could
25 image to himself Hastings the Governor-General only

as the Hastings with whom he had rowed on the Thames and played in the cloister, and refused to believe that so good-tempered a fellow could have done any thing very wrong. His own life had been spent in praying, musing, and rhyming among the water-lilies of the °Ouse. He had preserved in no common measure the innocence of childhood. His spirit had indeed been severely tried, but not by °temptations which impelled him to any gross violations of the rules of social morality. He had never been attacked by combinations of powerful and deadly enemies. He had never been compelled to make a choice between °innocence and greatness, between crime and ruin. Firmly as he held in theory the doctrine of human depravity, his habits were such that he was unable to conceive how far from the path of right even kind and noble natures may be hurried by the rage of conflict and the lust of dominion.

Hastings had another associate at Westminster of whom we shall have occasion to make frequent mention, Elijah Impey. We know little about their school days. But, we think, we may safely venture to guess that, whenever Hastings wished to play any trick more than usually naughty, he hired Impey with a tart or a ball to act as fag in the worst part of the prank.

Warren was distinguished among his comrades as an excellent swimmer, boatman, and scholar. At fourteen he was first in the examination for the °foundation. His name in gilded letters on the walls of the dormitory still attests his victory over many older competitors. He stayed two years longer at the school, and was looking forward to a °studentship at Christ Church, when an event happened which changed the whole course of his life. Howard Hastings died, bequeathing his nephew to the care of a friend and distant relation, named Chiswick. This gentleman, though he did not absolutely refuse the charge, was desirous to rid himself of it as soon as possible. Dr. Nichols made strong remonstrances against the cruelty of interrupting the studies of a youth who seemed likely to be one of the first scholars of the age. He even offered to bear the expense of sending his favorite pupil to Oxford. But Mr. Chiswick was inflexible. He thought the years which had already been wasted on °hexameters and pentameters quite sufficient. He had it in his power to obtain for the lad a °writership in the service of the °East India Company. Whether the young adventurer, when once shipped off, made a fortune, or died of a liver complaint, he equally ceased to be a burden to any body. Warren was accordingly removed from Westminster school, and placed for a few months at a commercial academy, to study arithmetic and book-keeping. In January, 1750, a few days after he had completed his seventeenth year, he sailed for Bengal, and arrived at his destination in the October following.

He was immediately placed at a desk in the Secretary's office at Calcutta, and labored there during two years. Fort William was then a purely commercial settlement. In the south of India the encroaching policy of °Dupleix had transformed the servants of the English company, against their will, into diplomatists and generals. °The war of the succession was raging in the Carnatic; and the tide had been suddenly turned against the French by the genius of young Robert Clive. But in Bengal the European settlers, at peace with the natives and with each other, were wholly occupied with ledgers and bills of lading.

After two years passed in keeping accounts at Calcutta, Hastings was sent up the country to Cossimbazar, a town which lies on the Hoogley, about a mile from Moorshedabad, and which then bore to Moorshedabad a relation, if we may compare small things with great, such as the city of London bears to Westminster. Moorshedabad was the abode of the °prince who, by an authority ostensibly derived from the Mogul, but really independent, ruled the three great provinces of Bengal, Orissa, and Bahar. At Moorshedabad were the court, the harem, and the public offices. Cossimbazar 5 was a port and a place of trade, renowned for the quantity and excellence of the silks which were sold in its marts, and constantly receiving and sending forth fleets of richly laden barges. At this important point, the Company had established a small factory 10 subordinate to that of Fort William. Here, during several years, Hastings was employed in making bargains for stuffs with native brokers. While he was thus engaged, Surajah Dowlah succeeded to the government, and declared war against the English. The 15 defenceless settlement of Cossimbazar, lying close to the tyrant's capital, was instantly seized. Hastings was sent a prisoner to Moorshedabad, but, in consequence of the humane intervention of the servants of the Dutch Company, was treated with indulgence. Meanwhile the 20 Nabob marched on Calcutta; the governor and the commandant fled; the town and citadel were taken, and most of the English prisoners perished in the °Black Hole.

In these events originated the greatness of Warren Hastings. The fugitive governor and his companions 25 had taken refuge on the dreary islet of Fulda, near the mouth of the Hoogley. They were naturally desirous to obtain full information respecting the proceedings of the Nabob; and no person seemed so likely to furnish it as Hastings, who was a prisoner at large in the immediate neighborhood of the court. He thus became a diplomatic agent, and soon established a high character for ability and resolution. The °treason which at a later period was fatal to Surajah Dowlah was already in progress; and Hastings was admitted to the deliberations of the conspirators. But the time for striking had not arrived. It was necessary to postpone the execution of the design; and Hastings, who was now in extreme peril, fled to Fulda.

Soon after his arrival at Fulda, the expedition from Madras, commanded by Clive, appeared in the Hoogley. Warren, young, intrepid, and excited probably by the example of the Commander of the Forces, who, having like himself been a mercantile agent of the Company, had been turned by public calamities into a soldier, determined to serve in the ranks. During the early operations of the war he carried a musket. But the quick eye of Clive soon perceived that the head of the young volunteer would be more useful than his arm. When, after the battle of Plassey, Meer Jaffier was proclaimed Nabob of Bengal, Hastings was

appointed to reside at the court of the new prince as
agent for the Company.

°He remained at Moorshedabad till the year 1761,
when he became a member of Council, and was conse-
quently forced to reside at Calcutta. This was during
the interval between Clive's first and second administration, an interval which has left on the fame of the
East India Company a stain, not wholly effaced by
many years of just and humane government. °Mr.
Vansittart, the Governor, was at the head of a new
and anomalous empire. On the one side was a band
of English functionaries, daring, intelligent, eager to
be rich. On the other side was a great native population, helpless, timid, accustomed to crouch under
oppression. To keep the stronger race from preying
on the weaker, was an undertaking which tasked
to the utmost the talents and energy of Clive. Vansittart, with fair intentions, was a feeble and inefficient
ruler. The master caste, as was natural, broke loose
from all restraint ; and then was seen what we believe
to be the most frightful of all spectacles, the strength
of civilization without its mercy. To all other despot-
ism there is a check, imperfect indeed, and liable to
gross abuse, but still sufficient to preserve society from
the last extreme of misery. A time comes when the

evils of submission are obviously greater than those
of resistance, when fear itself begets a sort of courage,
when a convulsive burst of popular rage and despair
warns tyrants not to presume too far on the patience
of mankind.   But against misgovernment such as 5
then afflicted Bengal it was impossible to struggle.
The superior intelligence and energy of the dominant
class made their power irresistible.   A war of Bengalees against Englishmen was like a war of sheep
against wolves, of men against demons.   The only 10
protection which the conquered could find was in the
moderation, the clemency, the enlarged policy of
the conquerers.   That protection, at a later period, they
found.   But at first English power came among them
unaccompanied by English morality.   There was an 1
interval between the time at which they became our
subjects, and the time at which we began to reflect
that we were bound to discharge towards them the
duties of rulers.   During that interval the business of
vant of the Company was simply to wring out of
natives a hundred or two hundred thous
s as speedily as possible, that he might re
before his constitution had suffered from the
rry a peer's daughter, to buy °rotten boro
wall, and to give balls in St. James's S

Of the conduct of Hastings at this time little is
known; but the little that is known, and the circumstance that little is known, must be considered
as honorable to him.   He could not protect the
5 natives: all that he could do was to abstain from
plundering and oppressing them; and this he appears
to have done.   °It is certain that at this time he
continued poor; and it is equally certain that by
cruelty and dishonesty he might easily have become
10 rich.   It is certain that he was never charged with
having borne a share in the worst abuses which then
prevailed; and it is almost equally certain that, if he
had borne a share in those abuses, the able and bitter
enemies who afterwards persecuted him would not
5 have failed to discover and to proclaim his guilt.
°The keen, severe, and even malevolent scrutiny
to which his whole public life was subjected, a scrutiny unparalleled, as we believe, in the history of
mankind, is in one respect advantageous to his reputation.   It brought many lamentable blemishes to l[ ]
it entitles him to be considered pure from
[ ]ish which has not been brought to light.
[ ]e truth is that the temptations to which s[ ]
[ ]ish functionaries yielded in the time of M[ ]
[ ]t were not temptations addressed to the[ ]

passions of Warren Hastings. He was not squeamish
in pecuniary transactions; but he was neither sordid
nor rapacious. He was far too enlightened a man to
look on a great empire merely as a buccaneer would
look on a galleon. Had his heart been much worse 5
than it was, his understanding would have preserved
him from that extremity of baseness. He was an
unscrupulous, perhaps an unprincipled, statesman;
but still he was a statesman, and not a freebooter.

In 1764 Hastings returned to England. He had 10
realized only a very moderate fortune; and that moderate fortune was soon reduced to nothing, partly by
his praiseworthy liberality, and partly by his mismanagement. Towards his relations he appears to have
acted very generously. The greater part of his sav- 15
ings he left in Bengal, hoping probably to obtain the
high usury of India. But high usury and bad security generally go together; and Hastings lost both
interest and principal.

He remained four years in England. Of his life at 20
this time very little is known. But it has been
asserted, and is highly probable, that liberal studies
and the society of men of letters occupied a great part
of his time. It is to be remembered to his honor that,
in days when the languages of the East were regarded 25

by other servants of the Company merely as the
means of communicating with weavers and money-
changers, his enlarged and accomplished mind sought
in Asiatic learning for new forms of intellectual enjoyment, and for new views of government and society.
Perhaps, like most persons who have paid much attention to departments of knowledge which lie out of the
common track, he was inclined to overrate the value
of his favorite studies.   He conceived that the culti-
vation of Persian literature might with advantage be
made a part of the liberal education of an English
gentleman; and he drew up a plan with that view.
It is said that the University of Oxford, in which
Oriental learning had never, since the revival of letters, been wholly neglected, was to be the seat of the
institution which he contemplated.   An endowment
was expected from the munificence of the Company:
and professors thoroughly competent to interpret
°Hafiz and Ferdusi were to be engaged in the East.
Hastings called on Johnson, with the hope, as it
should seem, of interesting in this project a man who
enjoyed the highest literary reputation, and who was
particularly connected with Oxford.   The interview
appears to have left on Johnson's mind a most favorable impression of the talents and attainments of his

visitor. Long after, when Hastings was ruling the immense population of British India, the old philosopher wrote to him, and referred in the most courtly terms, though with great dignity, to their short but agreeable intercourse.

Hastings soon began to look again towards India. He had little to attach him to England; and his pecuniary embarrassments were great. He solicited his old masters the Directors for employment. They acceded to his request, with high compliments both to his abilities and to his integrity, and appointed him a Member of Council at Madras. It would be unjust not to mention that, though forced to borrow money for his outfit, he did not withdraw any portion of the sum which he had appropriated to the relief of his distressed relations. In the spring of 1769 he embarked on board of the Duke of Grafton, and commenced a voyage distinguished by incidents which might furnish matter for a novel.

Among the passengers in the Duke of Grafton was a German of the name of Imhoff. He called himself a Baron; but he was in distressed circumstances, and was going out to Madras as a portrait-painter, in the hope of picking up some of the °pagodas which were then lightly got and as lightly spent by the En

c

in India.   The Baron was accompanied by his wife, a
native, we have somewhere read, of Archangel.   This
young woman who, born under the Arctic circle, was
destined to play the part of a Queen under the tropic
5 of Cancer, had an agreeable person, a cultivated mind,
and manners in the highest degree engaging.   She
despised her husband heartily, and, as the story which
we have to tell sufficiently proves, not without reason.
She was interested by the conversation and flattered
10 by the attentions of Hastings.   The situation was
indeed perilous.   No place is so propitious to the formation either of close friendships or of deadly enmities as an °Indiaman.   There are very few people who
do not find a voyage which lasts several months insup-
15 portably dull.   Any thing is welcome which may
break that long monotony, a sail, a shark, an albatross,
a man overboard.   Most passengers find some resource
in eating twice as many meals as on land.   But the
great devices for killing the time are quarrelling
and flirting.   The facilities for both these exciting
pursuits are great.   The inmates of the ship are
thrown together far more than in any country-seat
a boarding-house.   None can escape from the rest
pt by imprisoning himself in a cell in which he
hardly turn.   All food, all exercise, is taken in

company.   Ceremony is to a great extent banished.
It is every day in the power of a mischievous person
to inflict innumerable annoyances.   It is every day in
the power of an amiable person to confer little services.   It not seldom happens that serious distress 5
and danger call forth, in °genuine beauty and deform-
ity, heroic virtues and abject vices which, in the ordinary intercourse of good society, might remain during
many years unknown even to intimate associates.
Under such circumstances met Warren Hastings and 10
the Baroness Imhoff, two persons whose accomplishments would have attracted notice in any court of
Europe.   The gentleman had no domestic ties.   The
lady was tied to a husband for whom she had no
regard, and who had no regard for his own honor. 15
An attachment sprang up, which was soon strength-
ened by events such as could hardly have occurred on
land.   Hastings fell ill.   The Baroness nursed him
with womanly tenderness, gave him his medicines
with her own hand, and even sat up in his cabin while 20
he slept.   Long before the Duke of Grafton reached
Madras, Hastings was in love.   But his love was of a
most characteristic description.   Like his hatred, like
his ambition, like all his passions, it was strong, but
not impetuous.   It was calm, deep, earnest, patient 25

of delay, unconquerable by time.   Imhoff was called
into council by his wife and his wife's lover.   It was
arranged that the Baroness should institute a suit for
a divorce in the courts of Franconia, that the Baron
5 should afford every facility to the proceeding, and
that, during the years which might elapse before the
sentence should be pronounced, they should continue
to live together.   It was also agreed that Hastings
should bestow some very substantial marks of grati-
10 tude on the complaisant husband, and should, when
the marriage was dissolved, make the lady his wife,
and adopt the children whom she had already borne
to Imhoff.

At Madras, Hastings found the trade of the Com-
15 pany in a very disorganized state.   His own tastes
would have led him rather to political than to commercial pursuits : but he knew that the favor of his
employers depended chiefly on their dividends, and
that their dividends depended chiefly on the invest-
20 ment.   He therefore, with great judgment, determined
to apply his vigorous mind for a time to this department of business, which had been much neglected,
since the servants of the Company had ceased to be
clerks, and had become warriors and negotiators.
25 In a very few months he effected an important

decide between conflicting pretensions. Two candidates stood out prominently from the crowd, each of them the representative of a race and of a religion. One of these was Mahommed Reza °Khan, a Mussulman of Persian extraction, able, active, religious after the fashion of his people, and highly esteemed by them. In England he might perhaps have been regarded as a corrupt and greedy politician. But, tried by the lower standard of Indian morality, he might be considered as a man of integrity and honor. His competitor was a °Hindoo Brahmin whose name has, by a terrible and melancholy event, been inseparably associated with that of Warren Hastings, the °Maharajah Nuncomar. This man had played an important part in all the revolutions which, since the time of Surajah Dowlah, had taken place in Bengal. To the consideration which in that country belongs to high and pure caste, he added the weight which is derived from wealth, talents, and experience. Of his moral character it is difficult to give a notion to those who are acquainted with human nature only as it appears in our island. What the Italian is to the Englishman, what the Hindoo is to the Italian, what the Bengalee is to other Hindoos, that was Nuncomar to other Bengalees. The physical organization of the Ben-

galee is feeble even to effeminacy. He lives in a
constant vapor bath. His pursuits are sedentary, his
limbs delicate, his movements languid. During many
ages he has been trampled upon by men of bolder and
more hardy breeds. Courage, independence, verac-
ity, are qualities to which his constitution and his
situation are equally unfavorable. His mind bears a
singular analogy to his body. It is weak even to help-
lessness for purposes of manly resistance; but its sup-
pleness and its tact move the children of sterner
climates to admiration not unmingled with contempt.
All those arts which are the natural defence of the
weak are more familiar to this subtle race than to
the Ionian of the time of Juvenal, or to the Jew of the
dark ages. What the horns are to the buffalo, what
the paw is to the tiger, what the sting is to the bee,
what beauty, according to the old Greek song, is to
woman, deceit is to the Bengalee. Large promises,
smooth excuses, elaborate tissues of circumstantial
falsehood, chicanery, perjury, forgery, are the weapons, offensive and defensive, of the people of the
Lower Ganges. All those millions do not furnish one
°sepoy to the armies of the Company. But as usurers,
as money-changers, as sharp legal practitioners, no
class of human beings can bear a comparison with

them. With all his softness, the Bengalee is by no means placable in his enmities or prone to pity. The pertinacity with which he adheres to his purposes yields only to the immediate pressure of fear. Nor does he lack a certain kind of courage which is often wanting to his masters. To inevitable evils he is sometimes found to oppose a passive fortitude, such as the Stoics attributed to their ideal sage. A European warrior, who rushes on a battery of cannon with a loud hurrah, will sometimes shriek under the surgeon's knife, and fall into an agony of despair at the sentence of death. But the Bengalee, who would see his country overrun, his house laid in ashes, his children murdered or dishonored, without having the spirit to strike one blow, has yet been known to endure torture with the firmness of °Mucius, and to mount the scaffold with the steady step and even pulse of °Algernon Sidney.

In Nuncomar, the national character was strongly and with exaggeration personified. The Company's servants had repeatedly detected him in the most criminal intrigues. On one occasion he brought a false charge against another Hindoo, and tried to substantiate it by producing forged documents. On another occasion it was discovered that, while professing the strongest attachment to the English, he was engaged in several conspiracies against them, and in particular that he was the medium of a correspondence between the court of Delhi and the French authorities in the Carnatic. For these and similar practices he had been long detained in confinement. But his talents and influence had not only procured his liberation, but had obtained for him a certain degree of consideration even among the British rulers of his country.

Clive was extremely unwilling to place a Mussulman at the head of the administration of Bengal. On the other hand, he could not bring himself to confer immense power on a man to whom every sort of villany had repeatedly been brought home. Therefore, though the nabob, over whom Nuncomar had by intrigue acquired great influence, begged that the artful Hindoo might be intrusted with the government, Clive, after some hesitation, decided honestly and wisely in favor of Mahommed Reza Khan. When Hastings became Governor, Mahommed Reza Khan had held power seven years. An infant son of Meer Jaffier was now nabob; and the guardianship of the young prince's person had been confided to the minister.

Nuncomar, stimulated at once by cupidity and malice, had been constantly attempting to hurt the reputation of his successful rival. This was not difficult. The revenues of Bengal, under the administration established by Clive, did not yield such a surplus as had been anticipated by the Company; for, at that time, the most absurd notions were entertained in England respecting the wealth of India. Palaces of porphyry, hung with the richest brocade, heaps of pearls and diamonds, vaults from which pagodas and gold mohurs were measured out by the bushel, filled the imagination even of men of business. Nobody seemed to be aware of what nevertheless was most undoubtedly the truth, that India was a poorer country than countries which in Europe are reckoned poor, than Ireland, for example, or than Portugal. It was confidently believed by Lords of the Treasury and members for the city that Bengal would not only defray its own charges, but would afford an increased dividend to the proprietors of India stock, and large relief to the English finances. These absurd expectations were disappointed; and the °Directors, naturally enough, chose to attribute the disappointment rather to the mismanagement of Mahommed Reza Khan than to their own ignorance of the country intrusted to

their care. They were confirmed in their error by
the agents of Nuncomar; for Nuncomar had agents
even in °Leadenhall Street. Soon after Hastings
reached Calcutta, he received a letter addressed by
5 the Court of Directors, not to the council generally,
but to himself in particular. He was directed to remove Mahommed Reza Khan, to arrest him, together
with all his family and all his partisans, and to institute a strict inquiry into the whole administration of
10 the province. It was added that the Governor would
do well to avail himself of the assistance of Nuncomar in the investigation. The vices of Nuncomar
were acknowledged. But even from his vices, it was
said, much advantage might at such a conjuncture be
15 derived; and, though he could not safely be trusted,
it might still be proper to encourage him by hopes of
reward.

The Governor bore no good will to Nuncomar.
Many years before, they had known each other at
20 Moorshedabad; and then a quarrel had arisen between
them which all the authority of their superiors could
hardly compose. Widely as they differed in most
points, they resembled each other in this, that both
were men of unforgiving natures. To Mahommed
25 Reza Khan, on the other hand, Hastings had no feel-

ings of hostility. Nevertheless he proceeded to execute the instructions of the Company with an alacrity which he never showed, except when instructions were in perfect conformity with his own views. He had, wisely as we think, determined to get rid of the system of double government in Bengal. The orders of the Directors furnished him with the means of effecting his purpose, and dispensed him from the necessity of discussing the matter with his Council. He took his measures with his usual vigor and dexterity. At midnight, the palace of Mahommed Reza Khan at Moorshedabad was surrounded by a battalion of sepoys. The minister was roused from his slumbers and informed that he was a prisoner. With the Mussulman gravity, he bent his head and submitted himself to the will of God. He fell not alone. A chief named Schitab Roy had been intrusted with the government of Bahar. His valor and his attachment to the English had more than once been signally proved. On that memorable day on which the people of Patna saw from their walls the whole army of the Mogul scattered by the little band of Captain Knox, the voice of the British conquerors assigned the palm of gallantry to the brave Asiatic. " I never," said Knox, when he introduced Schitab

Roy, covered with blood and dust, to the English functionaries assembled in the factory, "I never saw a
native fight so before." Schitab Roy was involved in
the ruin of Mahommed Reza Khan, was removed from
office, and was placed under arrest. The members of
the Council received no intimation of these measures
till the prisoners were on their road to Calcutta.

The inquiry into the conduct of the minister was
postponed on different pretences. He was detained in
an easy confinement during many months. In the
mean time, the great revolution which Hastings had
planned was carried into effect. The office of minister
was abolished. The internal administration was transferred to the servants of the Company. A system,
a very imperfect system, it is true, of civil and criminal justice, under English superintendence, was established. The nabob was no longer to have even an
ostensible share in the government; but he was still
to receive a considerable annual allowance, and to be
surrounded with the state of sovereignty. As he was
an infant, it was necessary to provide guardians for
his person and property. His person was intrusted
to a lady of his father's harem, known by the name
of the Munny Begum. The office of treasurer of the
household was bestowed on a son of Nuncomar, named

Goordas. Nuncomar's services were wanted; yet he could not safely be trusted with power; and Hastings thought it a masterstroke of policy to reward the able and unprincipled parent by promoting the inoffensive child.

The revolution completed, the double government dissolved, the Company installed in the full sovereignty of Bengal, Hastings had no motive to treat the late ministers with rigor. Their trial had been put off on various pleas till the new organization was complete. They were then brought before a committee, over which the Governor presided. Schitab Roy was speedily acquitted with honor. A formal apology was made to him for the restraint to which he had been subjected. All the Eastern marks of respect were bestowed on him. He was clothed in a robe of state, presented with jewels and with a richly harnessed elephant, and sent back to his government at Patna. But his health had suffered from confinement; his high spirit had been cruelly wounded; and soon after his liberation he died of a broken heart.

The innocence of Mahommed Reza Khan was not so clearly established. But the Governor was not disposed to deal harshly. After a long hearing, in

D

which Nuncomar appeared as the accuser, and displayed both the art and the inveterate rancor which
distinguished him, Hastings pronounced that the
charges had not been made out, and ordered the fallen
5 minister to be set at liberty.

37 Nuncomar had purposed to destroy the Mussulman
administration, and to rise on its ruin. Both his
malevolence and his cupidity had been disappointed.
Hastings had made him a tool, had used him for the
10 purpose of accomplishing the transfer of the government from Moorshedabad to Calcutta, from native
to European hands. The rival, the enemy, so long
envied, so implacably persecuted, had been dismissed
unhurt. The situation so long and ardently desired
15 had been abolished. It was natural that the Governor should be from that time an object of the most
intense hatred to the vindictive Brahmin. As yet,
however, it was necessary to suppress such feelings.
The time was coming when that long animosity was
20 to end in a desperate and deadly struggle.

38 In the mean time, Hastings was compelled to turn
his attention to foreign affairs. The object of his
diplomacy was at this time simply to get money. The
finances of his government were in an embarrassed
25 state; and this embarrassment he was determined to

relieve by some means, fair or foul. The principle
which directed all his dealings with his neighbors is
fully expressed by the old motto of one of the great
predatory families of °Teviotdale, "Thou shalt want
ere I want." He seems to have laid it down, as a
fundamental proposition which could not be disputed,
that, when he had not as many lacs of rupees as the
public service required, he was to take them from any
body who had. One thing, indeed, is to be said in
excuse for him. The pressure applied to him by his
employers at home, was such as only the highest virtue
could have withstood, such as left him no choice except to commit great wrongs, or to resign his high
post, and with that post all his hopes of fortune and
distinction. The Directors, it is true, never enjoined
or applauded any crime. Far from it. Whoever
examines their letters written at that time will find
there many just and humane sentiments, many excellent precepts, in short, an admirable code of political
ethics. But every exhortation is modified or nullified
by a demand for money. "Govern leniently, and send
more money; practise strict justice and moderation
towards neighboring powers, and send more money;"
this is in truth the sum of almost all the instructions
that Hastings ever received from home. Now these

instructions, being interpreted, mean simply, " Be the father and the oppressor of the people; be just and unjust, moderate and rapacious." The Directors dealt with India, as the church, in the good old times, dealt
5 with a heretic. They delivered the victim over to the executioners, with an earnest request that all possible tenderness might be shown. We by no means accuse or suspect those who framed these despatches of hypocrisy. It is probable that, writing fifteen thou-
10 sand miles from the place where their orders were to be carried into effect, they never perceived the gross inconsistency of which they were guilty. But the inconsistency was at once manifest to their vicegerent at Calcutta, who, with an empty treasury, with an
15 unpaid army, with his own salary often in arrear, with deficient crops, with government tenants daily running away, was called upon to remit home another half million without fail. Hastings saw that it was absolutely necessary for him to disregard either the moral dis-
20 courses or the pecuniary requisitions of his employers. Being forced to disobey them in something, he had to consider what kind of disobedience they would most readily pardon; and he correctly judged that the safest course would be to neglect the °sermons and to
25 find the rupees.

39 A mind so fertile as his, and so little restrained by conscientious scruples, speedily discovered several modes of relieving the financial embarrassments of the government. The allowance of the Nabob of Bengal was reduced at a stroke from three hundred and twenty 5 thousand pounds a year to half that sum. The Company had bound itself to pay near three hundred thousand pounds a year to the Great Mogul, as a mark of homage for the provinces which he had intrusted to their care; and they had ceded to him the districts of 10 °Corah and Allahabad. On the plea that the Mogul was not really independent, but merely a tool in the hands of others, Hastings determined to retract these concessions. He accordingly declared that the English would pay no more tribute, and sent troops to 15 occupy Allahabad and Corah. The situation of these places was such, that there would be little advantage and great expense in retaining them. Hastings, who wanted money and not territory, determined to sell them. A purchaser was not wanting. The rich prov- 20 ince of Oude had, in the °general dissolution of the Mogul Empire, fallen to the share of the great Mussulman house by which it is still governed. About twenty years ago, this house, by the permission of the British government, °assumed the royal title; but, in 25

the time of Warren Hastings, such an assumption would have been considered by the Mahommedans of India as a monstrous impiety. The Prince of Oude, though he held the power, did not venture to use the
5 style of sovereignty. To the appellation of Nabob or Viceroy, he added that of Vizier of the monarchy of Hindostan, just as in the last century the Electors of Saxony and Brandenburg, though independent of the Emperor, and often in arms against him, were proud
10 to style themselves his Grand Chamberlain and Grand Marshal. Sujah Dowlah, then Nabob Vizier, was on excellent terms with the English. He had a large treasure. Allahabad and Corah were so situated that they might be of use to him and could be of none to
15 the Company. The buyer and seller soon came to an understanding; and the provinces which had been torn from the Mogul were made over to the government of Oude for about half a million sterling.

But there was another matter still more important
20 to be settled by the Vizier and the Governor. The fate of a brave people was to be decided. It was decided in a manner which has left a lasting stain on the fame of Hastings and of England.

The people of Central Asia had always been to the
25 inhabitants of India what the warriors of the German

forests were to the subjects of the decaying monarchy
of Rome. The dark, slender, and timid Hindoo shrank
from a conflict with the strong muscle and resolute
spirit of the fair race, which dwelt beyond their passes.
There is reason to believe that, at a period anterior to 5
the dawn of regular history, the people who spoke the
rich and flexible Sanscrit came from regions lying far
beyond the Hyphasis and the Hystaspes, and imposed
their yoke on the children of the soil. It is certain
that, during the last ten centuries, a succession of 10
invaders descended from the west on Hindostan; nor
was the course of conquest ever turned back towards
the setting sun, till that memorable campaign in which
the cross of Saint George was planted on the walls of
°Ghizni.

15

The Emperors of Hindostan themselves came from
the other side of the great mountain ridge; and it had
always been their practice to recruit their army from
the hardy and valiant race from which their own illustrious house sprang. Among the military adventur- 20
ers who were allured to the Mogul standards from
the neighborhood of Cabul and Candahar, were conspicuous several gallant bands, known by the name of
the °Rohillas. Their services had been rewarded with
large tracts of land, fiefs of the spear, if we may use 25

an expression drawn from an analogous state of things, in that fertile plain through which the Ramgunga flows from the snowy heights of Kumaon to join the Ganges. In the general confusion which followed the death of °Aurungzebe, the warlike colony became virtually independent. The Rohillas were distinguished from the other inhabitants of India by a peculiarly fair complexion. They were more honorably distinguished by courage in war, and by skill in the arts of peace. While anarchy raged from Lahore to Cape Comorin, their little territory enjoyed the blessings of repose under the guardianship of valor. Agriculture and commerce flourished among them; nor were they negligent of rhetoric and poetry. Many persons now living have heard aged men talk with regret of the golden days when the Afghan princes ruled in the vale of Rohilcund.

Sujah Dowlah had set his heart on adding this rich district to his own principality. Right or show of right, he had absolutely none. His claim was in no respect better founded than that of Catherine to Poland, or that of the Bonaparte family to Spain. The Rohillas held their country by exactly the same title by which he held his, and had governed their country far better than his had ever been governed.

Nor were they a people whom it was perfectly safe to attack. Their land was indeed an open plain destitute of natural defences; but their veins were full of the high blood of Afghanistan. As soldiers, they had not the steadiness which is seldom found except in company with strict discipline; but their impetuous valor had been proved on many fields of battle. It was said that their chiefs, when united by common peril, could bring eighty thousand men into the field. Sujah Dowlah had himself seen them fight, and wisely shrank from a conflict with them. There was in India one army, and only one, against which even those proud Caucasian tribes could not stand. It had been abundantly proved that neither tenfold odds, nor the martial ardor of the boldest Asiatic nations, could avail aught against English science and resolution. Was it possible to induce the Governor of Bengal to let out to hire the irresistible energies of the imperial people, the skill against which the ablest chiefs of Hindostan were helpless as infants, the discipline which had so often triumphed over the frantic struggles of fanaticism and despair, the unconquerable British courage which is never so sedate and stubborn as towards the close of a doubtful and murderous day?

This was what the Nabob Vizier asked, and what

Hastings granted. A bargain was soon struck. Each
of the negotiators had what the other wanted. Hastings was in need of funds to carry on the government
of Bengal, and to send remittances to London; and
5 Sujah Dowlah had an ample revenue. Sujah Dowlah
was bent on subjugating the Rohillas; and Hastings
had at his disposal the only force by which the
Rohillas could be subjugated. It was agreed that an
English army should be lent to the Nabob Vizier, and
10 that, for the loan, he should pay four hundred thousand
pounds sterling, besides defraying all the charge of the
troops while employed in his service.

"I really cannot see," says Mr. Gleig, "upon what
grounds, either of political or moral justice, this prop-
15 osition deserves to be stigmatized as infamous." If
we understand the meaning of words, it is infamous to
commit a wicked action for hire, and it is wicked to
engage in war without provocation. In this particular
war, scarcely one aggravating circumstance was want-
20 ing. The object of the Rohilla war was this, to
deprive a large population, who had never done us
the least harm, of a good government, and to place
them, against their will, under an execrably bad one.
Nay, even this is not all. England now descended far
25 below the level even of those petty German princes

who, about the same time, sold us troops to fight the
Americans. The hussar-mongers of Hesse and Anspach
had at least the assurance that the expeditions on
which their soldiers were to be employed would be conducted in conformity with the humane rules of civil- 5
ized warfare. Was the Rohilla war likely to be so
conducted? Did the Governor stipulate that it should
be so conducted? He well knew what Indian warfare
was. He well knew that the power which he cove-
nanted to put into Sujah Dowlah's hands would, in all 10
probability, be atrociously abused; and he required no
guarantee, no promise that it should not be so abused.
He did not even reserve to himself the right of with-
drawing his aid in case of abuse, however gross. We
are almost ashamed to notice Major Scott's absurd 15
plea, that Hastings was justified in letting out English
troops to slaughter the Rohillas, because the Rohillas
were not of Indian race, but a colony from a distant
country. What were the English themselves? Was
it for them to proclaim a crusade for the expulsion 20
of all intruders from the countries watered by the
Ganges? Did it lie in their mouths to contend that a
foreign settler who establishes an empire in India is
a *caput lupinum?* What would they have said if any
other power had, on such a ground, attacked Madras 25

or Calcutta without the slightest provocation? Such
a defence was wanting to make the infamy of the
transaction complete. The atrocity of the crime, and
the hypocrisy of the apology, are worthy of each
5 other.

One of the three brigades of which the Bengal
army consisted was sent under Colonel Champion to
join Sujah Dowlah's forces. The Rohillas expostu-
lated, entreated, offered a large ransom, but in vain.
10 They then resolved to defend themselves to the last.
A bloody battle was fought. "The enemy," says
Colonel Champion, "gave proof of a good share of
military knowledge; and it is impossible to describe
a more obstinate firmness of resolution than they dis-
15 played." The dastardly sovereign of Oude fled from
the field. The English were left unsupported; but
their fire and their charge were irresistible. It was
not, however, till the most distinguished chiefs had
fallen, fighting bravely at the head of their troops,
20 that the Rohilla ranks gave way. Then the Nabob
Vizier and his rabble made their appearance, and
hastened to plunder the camp of the valiant enemies,
whom they had never dared to look in the face. The
soldiers of the Company, trained in an exact disci-
25 pline, kept unbroken order, while the tents were pil·

laged by these worthless allies. But many voices
were heard to exclaim, "We have had all the fighting,
and those rogues are to have all the profit."

Then the horrors of Indian war were let loose on the
fair valleys and cities of Rohilcund. The whole country was in a blaze. More than a hundred thousand
people fled from their homes to pestilential jungles,
preferring famine, and fever, and the haunts of tigers,
to the tyranny of him, to whom an English and a
Christian government had, for shameful lucre, sold
their substance, and their blood, and the honor of
their wives and daughters. Colonel Champion re-
monstrated with the Nabob Vizier, and sent strong
representations to Fort William; but the Governor
had made no conditions as to the mode in which the
war was to be carried on. He had troubled himself
about nothing but his forty lacs; and, though he
might disapprove of Sujah Dowlah's wanton barbar-
ity, he did not think himself entitled to interfere,
except by offering advice. This delicacy excites the
admiration of the biographer. "Mr. Hastings," he
says, "could not himself dictate to the Nabob, nor
permit the commander of the Company's troops to
dictate how the war was to be carried on." No, to be
sure. Mr. Hastings had only to put down by main

force the brave struggles of innocent men fighting for their liberty. Their military resistance crushed, his duties ended; and he had then only to fold his arms and look on, while their villages were burned, their
5 children butchered, and their women violated. Will Mr. Gleig seriously maintain this opinion? Is any rule more plain than this, that whoever voluntarily gives to another irresistible power over human beings is bound to take order that such power shall not be
10 barbarously abused? But we beg pardon of our readers for arguing a point so clear.

We hasten to the end of this sad and disgraceful story. The war ceased. The finest population in India was subjected to a greedy, cowardly, cruel
15 tyrant. Commerce and agriculture languished. The rich province which had tempted the cupidity of Sujah Dowlah became the most miserable part even of his miserable dominions. Yet is the injured nation not extinct. At long intervals gleams of its ancient
20 spirit have flashed forth; and even at this day, valor, and self-respect, and a chivalrous feeling rare among Asiatics, and a bitter remembrance of the great crime of England, distinguish that noble Afghan race. To this day they are regarded as the best of all sepoys
25 at the cold steel; and it was very recently remarked,

by one who had enjoyed great opportunities of observation, that the only natives of India to whom the word "gentleman" can with perfect propriety be applied, are to be found among the Rohillas.

Whatever we may think of the morality of Hastings, it cannot be denied that the financial results of his policy did honor to his talents. In less than two years after he assumed the government, he had, without imposing any additional burdens on the people subject to his authority, added about four hundred and fifty thousand pounds to the annual income of the Company, besides procuring about a million in ready money. He had also relieved the finances of Bengal from military expenditure, amounting to near a quarter of a million a year, and had thrown that charge on the Nabob of Oude. There can be no doubt that this was a result which, if it had been obtained by honest means, would have entitled him to the warmest gratitude of his country, and which, by whatever means obtained, proved that he possessed great talents for administration.

In the mean time, Parliament had been engaged in long and grave discussions on Asiatic affairs. The ministry of Lord North, in the session of 1773, introduced a measure which made a considerable change in the constitution of the Indian government. This law, known by the name of °the Regulating Act, provided that the presidency of Bengal should exercise a control over the other possessions of the Company; that the chief of that presidency should be styled Governor-General; that he should be assisted by four Councillors; and that a supreme court of judicature, consisting of a chief justice and three inferior judges, should be established at Calcutta. This court was made independent of the Governor-General and Council, and was intrusted with a civil and criminal jurisdiction of immense and, at the same time, of undefined extent.

The Governor-General and Councillors were named in the act, and were to hold their situations for five years. Hastings was to be the first Governor-General. One of the four new Councillors, Mr. Barwell, an experienced servant of the Company, was then in India. The other three, General Clavering, Mr. Monson, and Mr. Francis, were sent out from England.

The ablest of the new Councillors was, beyond all doubt, Philip Francis. His acknowledged compositions prove that he possessed considerable eloquence and information. Several years passed in the public offices had formed him to habits of business. His enemies have never denied that he had a fearless and

manly spirit; and his friends, we are afraid, must
acknowledge that his estimate of himself was extrava-
gantly high, that his temper was irritable, that his
deportment was often rude and petulant, and that his
hatred was of intense bitterness and long duration. 5

It is scarcely possible to mention this eminent man
without adverting for a moment to the question which
his name at once suggests to every mind. Was he
the author of the °Letters of Junius ? Our own firm
belief is that he was. The evidence is, we think, such 10
as would support a verdict in a civil, nay, in a criminal
proceeding. The handwriting of Junius is the very
peculiar handwriting of Francis, slightly disguised.
As to the position, pursuits, and connections of Junius,
the following are the most important facts which can 15
be considered as clearly proved: first, that he was
acquainted with the technical forms of the secretary
of state's office; secondly, that he was intimately acquainted with the business of the war-office; thirdly,
that he, during the year 1770, attended debates in the 20
House of Lords, and took notes of speeches, particularly of the speeches of Lord Chatham; fourthly, that
he bitterly resented the appointment of Mr. Chamier
to the place of deputy secretary-at-war; fifthly, that
he was bound by some strong tie to the first Lord 25

E

Holland. Now, Francis passed some years in the
secretary of state's office. He was subsequently chief
clerk of the war-office. He repeatedly mentioned that
he had himself, in 1770, heard speeches of Lord
Chatham; and some of these speeches were actually
printed from his notes. He resigned his clerkship at
the war-office from resentment at the appointment of
Mr. Chamier. It was by Lord Holland that he was
first introduced into the public service. Now, here
are five marks, all of which ought to be found in
Junius. They are all five found in Francis. We do
not believe that more than two of them can be found
in any other person whatever. If this argument does
not settle the question, there is an end of all reasoning
on circumstantial evidence.

The internal evidence seems to us to point the same
way. The style of Francis bears a strong resemblance to that of Junius; nor are we disposed to
admit, what is generally taken for granted, that the
acknowledged compositions of Francis are very decidedly inferior to the anonymous letters. The argument from inferiority, at all events, is one which may
be urged with at least equal force against every claimant that has ever been mentioned, with the single exception of Burke; and it would be a waste of time to

prove that Burke was not Junius. And what conclusion, after all, can be drawn from mere inferiority? Every writer must produce his best work; and the interval between his best work and his second best work may be very wide indeed. Nobody will say that the best letters of Junius are more decidedly superior to the acknowledged works of Francis than three or four of Corneille's tragedies to the rest, than three or four of Ben Jonson's comedies to the rest, than the Pilgrim's Progress to the other works of Bunyan, than Don Quixote to the other works of Cervantes. Nay, it is certain that Junius, whoever he may have been, was a most unequal writer. To go no further than the letters which bear the signature of Junius; the letter to the King, and the letters to Horne Tooke, have little in common, except the asperity; and asperity was an ingredient seldom wanting either in the writings or in the speeches of Francis.

Indeed one of the strongest reasons for believing that Francis was Junius is the moral resemblance between the two men. It is not difficult, from the letters which, under various signatures, are known to have been written by Junius, and from his dealings with °Woodfall and others, to form a tolerably correct notion of his character. He was clearly a man not

destitute of real patriotism and magnanimity, a man whose vices were not of a sordid kind. But he must also have been a man in the highest degree arrogant and insolent, a man prone to malevolence, and prone
5 to the error of mistaking his malevolence for public virtue. °"Doest thou well to be angry?" was the question asked in old time of the Hebrew prophet And he answered, "I do well." This was evidently the temper of Junius; and to this cause we attribute
10 the savage cruelty which disgraces several of his letters. No man is so merciless as he who, under a strong self-delusion, confounds his antipathies with his duties. It may be added that Junius, though allied with the democratic party by common enmities,
15 was the very opposite of a democratic politician. While attacking individuals with a ferocity which perpetually violated all the laws of literary warfare, he regarded the most defective parts of old institutions with a respect amounting to pedantry, pleaded
20 the cause of °Old Sarum with fervor, and contemptuously told the capitalists of Manchester and Leeds that, if they wanted votes, they might buy land and become freeholders of Lancashire and Yorkshire. All this, we believe, might stand, with scarcely any change,
25 for a character of Philip Francis.

It is not strange that the great anonymous writer should have been willing at that time to leave the country which had been so powerfully stirred by his eloquence. Every thing had gone against him. That party which he clearly preferred to every other, the party of George Grenville, had been scattered by the death of its chief; and Lord Suffolk had led the greater part of it over to the ministerial benches. The ferment produced by the Middlesex election had gone down. Every faction must have been alike an object of aversion to Junius. His opinions on domestic affairs separated him from the ministry; his opinions on colonial affairs from the opposition. Under such circumstances, he had thrown down his pen in misanthropical despair. His farewell letter to Woodfall bears date the nineteenth of January 1773. In that letter, he declared that he must be an idiot to write again; that he had meant well by the cause and the public; that both were given up; that there were not ten men who would act steadily together on any question. "But it is all alike," he added, "vile and contemptible. You have never flinched that I know of; and I shall always rejoice to hear of your prosperity." These were the last words of Junius. In a year from that time, Philip Francis was on his voyage to Bengal.

With the three new Councillors came out the judges
of the Supreme Court. The chief justice was Sir
Elijah Impey. He was an old acquaintance of Hastings; and it is probable that the Governor-General, if
5 he had searched through all the °Inns of Court, could
not have found an equally serviceable tool. But the
members of Council were by no means in an obsequious mood. Hastings greatly disliked the new form
of government, and had no very high opinion of his
10 coadjutors. They had heard of this, and were disposed
to be suspicious and punctilious. When men are in
such a frame of mind, any trifle is sufficient to give
occasion for dispute. The members of Council expected
a salute of °twenty-one guns from the batteries of
15 Fort William. Hastings allowed them only seventeen.
They landed in ill-humor. The first civilities were
exchanged with cold reserve. On the morrow commenced that long quarrel which, after distracting
British India, was renewed in England, and in which
20 all the most eminent statesmen and orators of the age
took active part on one or the other side.

Hastings was supported by Barwell. They had not
always been friends. But the arrival of the new members of Council from England naturally had the effect
25 of uniting the old servants of the Company. Claver-

ing, Monson, and Francis formed the majority. They instantly wrested the government out of the hands of Hastings, condemned, certainly not without justice, his late dealings with the Nabob Vizier, recalled the English agent from Oude, and sent thither a creature of their own, ordered the brigade which had conquered the unhappy Rohillas to return to the Company's territories, and instituted a severe inquiry into the conduct of the war. Next, in spite of the Governor-General's remonstrances, they proceeded to exercise, in the most indiscreet manner, their new authority over the subordinate presidencies; threw all the affairs of °Bombay into confusion; and interfered, with an incredible union of rashness and feebleness, in the intestine disputes of the Mahratta government. At the same time, they fell on the internal administration of Bengal, and attacked the whole fiscal and judicial system, a system which was undoubtedly defective, but which it was very improbable that gentlemen fresh from England would be competent to amend. The effect of their reforms was that all protection to life and property was withdrawn, and that gangs of robbers plundered and slaughtered with impunity in the very suburbs of Calcutta. Hastings continued to live in the Government-house, and to draw the salary

of Governor-General. He continued even to take the
lead at the council-board in the transaction of ordinary
business; for his opponents could not but feel that he
knew much of which they were ignorant, and that he
decided, both surely and speedily, many questions
which to them would have been hopelessly puzzling.
But the higher powers of government and the most
valuable patronage had been taken from him.

The natives soon found this out. They considered
him as a fallen man; and they acted after their kind.
Some of our readers may have seen, in India, a cloud
of crows pecking a sick vulture to death, no bad type
of what happens in that country, as often as fortune
deserts one who has been great and dreaded. In an
instant, all the sycophants who had lately been ready
to lie for him, to forge for him, to pander for him, to
poison for him, hasten to purchase the favor of his
victorious enemies by accusing him. An Indian government has only to let it be understood that it wishes
a particular man to be ruined; and, in twenty-four
hours, it will be furnished with grave charges, supported by dispositions so full and circumstantial that
any person unaccustomed to Asiatic mendacity would
regard them as decisive. It is well if the signature of
the destined victim is not counterfeited at the foot of

some illegal compact, and if some treasonable paper is not slipped into a hiding-place in his house. Hastings was now regarded as helpless. The power to make or mar the fortune of every man in Bengal had passed, as it seemed, into the hands of the new Councillors. Immediately charges against the Governor-General began to pour in. They were eagerly welcomed by the majority, who, to do them justice, were men of too much honor knowingly to countenance false accusations, but who were not sufficiently acquainted with the East to be aware that, in that part of the world, a very little encouragement from power will call forth, in a week, more °Oateses, and Bedloes, and Danger-fields, than Westminster Hall sees in a century.

It would have been strange indeed if, at such a juncture, Nuncomar had remained quiet. That bad man was stimulated at once by malignity, by avarice, and by ambition. Now was the time to be avenged on his old enemy, to wreak a grudge of seventeen years, to establish himself in the favor of the majority of the Council, to become the greatest native in Bengal. From the time of the arrival of the new Councillors, he had paid the most marked court to them, and had in consequence been excluded, with all indignity, from the Government-house. He now put into the hands of

Francis, with great ceremony, a paper containing several charges of the most serious description. By this document Hastings was accused of putting offices up for sale, and of receiving bribes for suffering of-
5 fenders to escape. In particular, it was alleged that Mahommed Reza Khan had been dismissed with impunity, in consideration of a great sum paid to the Governor-General.

Francis read the paper in Council. A violent alter-
10 cation followed. Hastings complained in bitter terms of the way in which he was treated, spoke with con-tempt of Nuncomar and of Nuncomar's accusation, and denied the right of the Council to sit in judgment on the Governor. At the next meeting of the Board,
15 another communication from Nuncomar was produced. He requested that he might be permitted to attend the Council, and that he might be heard in support of his assertions. Another tempestuous debate took place. The Governor-General maintained that the council-
20 room was not a proper place for such an investiga-tion; that from persons who were heated by daily conflict with him he could not expect the fairness of judges; and that he could not, without betraying the dignity of his post, submit to be confronted with such
25 a man as Nuncomar. The majority, however, resolved

to go into the charges. Hastings rose, declared the sitting at an end, and left the room, followed by Barwell. The other members kept their seats, voted themselves a council, put Clavering in the chair, and ordered Nuncomar to be called in. Nuncomar not only adhered to the original charges, but, after the fashion of the East, produced a large supplement. He stated that Hastings had received a great sum for appointing Rajah Goordas treasurer of the Nabob's household, and for committing the care of his Highness's person to the °Munny Begum. He put in a letter purporting to bear the seal of the Munny Begum, for the purpose of establishing the truth of his story. The seal, whether forged, as Hastings affirmed, or genuine, as we are rather inclined to believe, proved nothing. Nuncomar, as every body knows who knows India, had only to tell the Munny Begum that such a letter would give pleasure to the majority of the Council, in order to procure her attestation. The majority, however, voted that the charge was made out; that Hastings had corruptly received between thirty and forty thousand pounds; and that he ought to be compelled to refund.

The general feeling among the English in Bengal was strongly in favor of the Governor-General. In talents for business, in knowledge of the country, in

general courtesy of demeanor, he was decidedly superior to his persecutors. The servants of the Company were naturally disposed to side with the most distinguished member of their own body against a
5 clerk from the war-office, who, profoundly ignorant of the native languages and of the native character, took on himself to regulate every department of the administration. Hastings, however, in spite of the general sympathy of his countrymen, was in a most painful
10 situation. There was still an appeal to higher authority in England. If that authority took part with his enemies, nothing was left to him but to throw up his office. He accordingly placed his resignation in the hands of his agent in London, Colonel Macleane. But
15 Macleane was instructed not to produce the resignation unless it should be fully ascertained that the feeling at the India House was adverse to the Governor-General. The triumph of Nuncomar seemed to be complete. He held a daily levee, to which his countrymen
20 resorted in crowds, and to which, on one occasion, the majority of the Council condescended to repair. His house was an office for the purpose of receiving charges against the Governor-General. It was said that, partly by threats, and partly by wheedling, the
25 villanous Brahmin had induced many of the wealthi-

est men of the province to send in complaints. But he was playing a perilous game. It was not safe to drive to despair a man of such resources and such determination as Hastings. Nuncomar, with all his acuteness, did not understand the nature of the insti- tutions under which he lived. He saw that he had with him the majority of the body which made treaties, gave places, raised taxes. The separation between political and judicial functions was a thing of which he had no conception. It had probably never occurred to him that there was in Bengal an authority perfectly independent of the Council, an authority which could protect one whom the Council wished to destroy, and send to the gibbet one whom the Council wished to protect. Yet such was the fact. The Supreme Court was, within the sphere of its own duties, altogether independent of the Government. Hastings, with his usual sagacity, had seen how much advantage he might derive from possessing himself of this stronghold; and he had acted accordingly. The Judges, especially the Chief Justice, were hostile to the majority of the Council. The time had now come for putting this formidable machinery into action.

On a sudden, Calcutta was astounded by the news that Nuncomar had been taken up on a charge of felony, committed, and thrown into the common gaol. The crime imputed to him was that six years before he had forged a bond. The ostensible prosecutor was a native. But it was then, and still is, the opinion of everybody, idiots and biographers excepted, that Hastings was the real mover in the business.

The rage of the majority rose to the highest point. They protested against the proceedings of the Supreme Court, and sent several urgent messages to the Judges, demanding that Nuncomar should be admitted to bail. The Judges returned haughty and resolute answers. All that the Council could do was to heap honors and emoluments on the family of Nuncomar; and this they did. In the mean time the assizes commenced; a true bill was found; and Nuncomar was brought before Sir Elijah Impey and a jury composed of Englishmen. A great quantity of contradictory swearing, and the necessity of having every word of the evidence interpreted, protracted the trial to a most unusual length. At last a verdict of guilty was returned, and the Chief Justice pronounced sentence of death on the prisoner.

That Impey ought to have respited Nuncomar we hold to be perfectly clear. Whether the whole proceeding was not illegal, is a question. But it is certain that, whatever may have been, according to technical rules of construction, the effect of the statute under which the trial took place, it was most unjust to hang a Hindoo for forgery. The law which made forgery capital in England was passed without the smallest reference to the state of society in India. It was unknown to the natives of India. It had never been put in execution among them, certainly not for want of delinquents. It was in the highest degree shocking to all their notions. They were not accustomed to the distinction which many circumstances, peculiar to our own state of society, have led us to make between forgery and other kinds of cheating. The counterfeiting of a seal was, in their estimation, a common act of swindling; nor had it ever crossed their minds that it was to be punished as severely as gang-robbery or assassination. A just judge would, beyond all doubt, have reserved the case for the consideration of the sovereign. But Impey would not hear of mercy or delay.

The excitement among all classes was great. Francis and Francis's few English adherents described the Governor-General and the Chief Justice as the worst of murderers. Clavering, it was said, swore that, even at the foot of the gallows, Nuncomar

should be rescued.   The bulk of the European society,
though strongly attached to the Governor-General,
could not but feel compassion for a man who with all
his crimes, had so long filled so large a space in their
5 sight, who had been great and powerful before the
British empire in India began to exist, and to whom,
in the old times, governors and members of council,
then mere commercial factors, had paid court for protection.   The feeling of the Hindoos was infinitely
10 stronger.   They were, indeed, not a people to strike
one blow for their countryman.   But his sentence
filled them with sorrow and dismay.   Tried even by
their low standard of morality, he was a bad man.
But, bad as he was, he was the head of their race and
15 religion, a Brahmin of the Brahmins.   He had inherited the purest and highest caste.   He had practised with the greatest punctuality all those ceremonies
to which the °superstitious Bengalees ascribe far more
importance than to the correct discharge of the social
20 duties.   They felt, therefore, as a devout Catholic in
the dark ages would have felt, at seeing a prelate of
the highest dignity sent to the gallows by a secular
tribunal.   According to their old national laws, a
Brahmin could not be put to death for any crime
25 whatever.   And the crime for which Nuncomar was

about to die was regarded by them in much the same light in which the selling of an unsound horse, for a sound price, is regarded by a Yorkshire jockey.

The Mussulmans alone appear to have seen with exultation the fate of the powerful Hindoo, who had attempted to rise by means of the ruin of Mahommed Reza Khan. The Mahommedan historian of those times takes delight in aggravating the charge. He assures us that in Nuncomar's house a casket was found containing counterfeits of the seals of all the richest men of the province. We have never fallen in with any other authority for this story, which in itself is by no means improbable.

The day drew near; and Nuncomar prepared himself to die with that quiet fortitude with which the Bengalee, so effeminately timid in personal conflict, often encounters calamities for which there is no remedy. The sheriff, with the humanity which is seldom wanting in an English gentleman, visited the prisoner on the eve of the execution, and assured him that no indulgence, consistent with the law, should be refused to him. Nuncomar expressed his gratitude with great politeness and unaltered composure. Not a muscle of his face moved. Not a sigh broke from him. He put his finger to his forehead, and calmly

F

said that fate would have its way, and that there was no resisting the pleasure of God. He sent his compliments to Francis, Clavering, and Monson, and charged them to protect Rajah Goordas, who was about to become the head of the Brahmins of Bengal. The sheriff withdrew, greatly agitated by what had passed, and Nuncomar sat composedly down to write notes and examine accounts.

The next morning, before the sun was in his power, an immense concourse assembled round the place where the gallows had been set up. Grief and horror were on every face; yet to the last the multitude could hardly believe that the English really purposed to take the life of the great Brahmin. At length the mournful procession came through the crowd. Nuncomar sat up in his palanquin, and looked round him with unaltered serenity. He had just parted from those who were most nearly connected with him. Their cries and contortions had appalled the European ministers of justice, but had not produced the smallest effect on the iron stoicism of the prisoner. The only anxiety which he expressed was that men of his own priestly caste might be in attendance to take charge of his corpse. He again desired to be remembered to his friends in the Council, mounted the scaffold with firmness, and gave the signal to the executioner. The moment that the drop fell, a howl of sorrow and despair rose from the innumerable spectators. Hundreds turned away their faces from the polluting sight, fled with loud wailings towards the Hoogley, and plunged into its °holy waters, as if to purify themselves from the guilt of having looked on such a crime. These feelings were not confined to Calcutta. The whole province was greatly excited; and the population of Decca, in particular, gave strong signs of grief and dismay.

Of Impey's conduct it is impossible to speak too severely. We have already said that, in our opinion, he acted unjustly in refusing to respite Nuncomar. No rational man can doubt that he took this course in order to gratify the Governor-General. If we had ever had any doubts on that point, they would have been dispelled by a letter which Mr. Gleig has published. Hastings, three or four years later, described Impey as the man "to whose support he was at one time indebted for the safety of his fortune, honor, and reputation." These strong words can refer only to the case of Nuncomar; and they must mean that Impey hanged Nuncomar in order to support Hastings. °It is, therefore, our deliberate opinion that Impey,

sitting as a judge, put a man unjustly to death in order
to serve a political purpose.

But we look on the conduct of Hastings in a somewhat different light. He was struggling for fortune,
honor, liberty, all that makes life valuable. He was
beset by rancorous and unprincipled enemies. From
his colleagues he could expect no justice. He cannot
be blamed for wishing to crush his accusers. He was
indeed bound to use only legitimate means for that
end. But it was not strange that he should have
thought any means legitimate which were pronounced
legitimate by the sages of the law, by men whose
peculiar duty it was to deal justly between adversaries, and whose education might be supposed to
have peculiarly qualified them for the discharge of
that duty. Nobody demands from a party the unbend-
ing equity of a judge. The reason that judges are
appointed is, that even a good man cannot be trusted
to decide a cause in which he is himself concerned.
Not a day passes on which an honest prosecutor does
not ask for what none but a dishonest tribunal would
grant. It is too much to expect that any man, when
his dearest interests are at stake, and his strongest
passions excited, will, as against himself, be more just
than the sworn dispensers of justice. To take an anal-

ogous case from the history of our own island: suppose
that Lord Stafford, when in the Tower on suspicion of
being concerned in the Popish plot, had been apprised
that Titus Oates had done something which might,
by a questionable construction, be brought under the
head of felony.   Should we severely blame Lord
Stafford, in the supposed case, for causing a prosecution to be instituted, for furnishing funds, for using all
his influence to intercept the mercy of the Crown?   We
think not.   If a judge, indeed, from favor to the Catholic lords, were to strain the law in order to hang Oates,
such a judge would richly deserve impeachment.   But
it does not appear to us that the Catholic lord, by
bringing the case before the judge for decision, would
materially overstep the limits of a just self-defence.
While, therefore, we have not the least doubt that
this memorable execution is to be attributed to Hastings, we doubt whether it can with justice be reckoned
among his crimes.   That his conduct was dictated by
a profound policy is evident.   He was in a minority
in Council.   It was possible that he might long be in
a minority.   He knew the native character well.   He
knew in what abundance accusations are certain to
flow in against the most innocent inhabitant of India
who is under the frown of power.   There was not in

the whole black population of Bengal a °place-holder,
a °place-hunter, a government tenant, who did not
think that he might better himself by sending up a
deposition against the Governor-General.　　Under
these circumstances, the persecuted statesman resolved
to teach the whole crew of accusers and witnesses
that, though in a minority at the council-board, he
was still to be feared.　The lesson which he gave
them was indeed a lesson not to be forgotten.　The
head of the combination which had been formed
against him, the richest, the most powerful, the most
artful of the Hindoos, distinguished by the favor of
those who then held the government, fenced round by
the superstitious reverence of millions, was hanged in
broad day before many thousands of people.　Every
thing that could make the warning impressive, dignity
in the sufferer, solemnity in the proceeding, was found
in this case.　The helpless rage and vain struggles of
the Council made the triumph more signal.　From
that moment the conviction of every native was that
it was safer to take the part of Hastings in a minority
than that of Francis in a majority, and that he who
was so venturous as to join in running down the
Governor-General might chance, in the phrase of the
Eastern poet, to find a tiger, while beating the jungle

for a deer. The voices of a thousand informers were silenced in an instant. From that time, whatever difficulties Hastings might have to encounter, he was never molested by accusations from natives of India. It is a remarkable circumstance that one of the letters of Hastings to Dr. Johnson bears date a very few hours after the death of Nuncomar. While the whole settlement was in commotion, while a mighty and ancient priesthood were weeping over the remains of their chief, the conqueror in that deadly grapple sat down, with characteristic self-possession, to write about the Tour to the Hebrides, °Jones's Persian Grammar, and the history, traditions, arts, and natural productions of India.

In the mean time, intelligence of the Rohilla war, and of the first disputes between Hastings and his colleagues, had reached London. The Directors took part with the majority, and sent out a letter filled with severe reflections on the conduct of Hastings. They condemned, in strong but just terms, the iniquity of undertaking offensive wars merely for the sake of pecuniary advantage. But they entirely forgot that, if Hastings had by illicit means obtained pecuniary advantages, he had done so, not for his own benefit, but in order to meet their demands. To enjoin

honesty, and to insist on having what could not be
honestly got, was then the constant practice of the
Company. As Lady Macbeth says of her husband,
they "would not play false, and yet would wrongly
5 win."

The Regulating Act, by which Hastings had been
appointed Governor-General for five years, empowered
the Crown to remove him on an address from the
Company. °Lord North was desirous to procure such
10 an address. The three members of Council who had
been sent out from England were men of his own
choice. General Clavering, in particular, was supported by a large parliamentary connection, such as
no cabinet could be inclined to disoblige. The wish
15 of the minister was to displace Hastings, and to put
Clavering at the head of the government. In the
Court of Directors parties were very nearly balanced.
Eleven voted against Hastings; ten for him. The
Court of Proprietors was then convened. The great
20 sale-room presented a singular appearance. Letters
had been sent by the Secretary of the Treasury, ex-
horting all the supporters of government who held
India stock to be in attendance. Lord Sandwich
marshalled the friends of the administration with his
25 usual dexterity and alertness. Fifty peers and privy

councillors, seldom seen so far eastward, were counted
in the crowd. The debate lasted till midnight. The
opponents of Hastings had a small superiority on the
division; but a ballot was demanded; and the result
was that the Governor-General triumphed by a ma- 5
jority of above a hundred votes over the combined
efforts of the Directors and the Cabinet. The ministers were greatly exasperated by this defeat. Even
Lord North lost his temper, no ordinary occurrence
with him, and threatened to convoke Parliament before 10
Christmas, and to bring in a bill for depriving the
Company of all political power, and for restricting
it to its old business of trading in silks and teas.

Colonel Macleane, who through all this conflict
had zealously supported the cause of Hastings, now 15
thought that his employer was in imminent danger of
being turned out, branded with parliamentary censure,
perhaps prosecuted. The opinion of the crown lawyers had already been taken respecting some parts
of the Governor-General's conduct. It seemed to be 20
high time to think of securing an honorable retreat.
Under these circumstances, Macleane thought himself
justified in producing the resignation with which he
had been entrusted. The instrument was not in very
accurate form; but the Directors were too eager to 25

be scrupulous. They accepted the resignation, fixed
on Mr. Wheler, one of their own body, to succeed
Hastings, and sent out orders that General Clavering,
as senior member of Council, should exercise the
functions of Governor-General till Mr. Wheler should
arrive.

But, while these things were passing in England,
a great change had taken place in Bengal. Monson
was no more. Only four members of the government
were left. Clavering and Francis were on one side,
Barwell and the Governor-General on the other; and
the Governor-General had the casting vote. Hastings,
who had been during two years destitute of all power
and patronage, became at once absolute. He instantly
proceeded to retaliate on his adversaries. Their
measures were reversed: their creatures were dis-
placed. A new valuation of the lands of Bengal, for
the purposes of taxation, was ordered: and it was
provided that the whole inquiry should be conducted
by the Governor-General, and that all the letters relating to it should run in his name. He began, at
the same time, to revolve vast plans of conquest and
dominion, plans which he lived to see realized, though
not by himself. His project was to form subsidiary
alliances with the native princes, particularly with

those of Oude and Berar, and thus to make Britain the paramount power in India. While he was meditating these great designs, arrived the intelligence that he had ceased to be Governor-General, that his resignation had been accepted, that Wheler was coming out immediately, and that, till Wheler arrived, the chair was to be filled by Clavering.

Had Hastings still been in a minority, he would probably have retired without a struggle; but he was now the real master of British India, and he was not disposed to quit his high place. He asserted that he had never given any instructions which could warrant the steps taken at home. What his instructions had been, he owned he had forgotten. If he had kept a copy of them he had mislaid it. But he was certain that he had repeatedly declared to the Directors that he would not resign. He could not see how the court, possessed of that declaration from himself, could receive his resignation from the doubtful hands of an agent. If the resignation were invalid, all the proceedings which were founded on that resignation were null, and Hastings was still Governor-General.

He afterwards affirmed that, though his agents had not acted in conformity with his instructions, he would nevertheless have held himself bound by their acts, if Clavering had not attempted to seize the supreme power by violence. Whether this assertion were or were not true, it cannot be doubted that the imprudence of Clavering gave Hastings an advantage. The General sent for the keys of the fort and of the treasury, took possession of the records, and held a council at which Francis attended. Hastings took the chair in another apartment, and Barwell sat with him. Each of the two parties had a plausible show of right. There was no authority entitled to their obedience within fifteen thousand miles. It seemed that there remained no way of settling the dispute except an appeal to arms; and from such an appeal Hastings, confident of his influence over his countrymen in India, was not inclined to shrink. He directed the officers of the garrison at Fort William and of all the neighboring stations to obey no orders but his. At the same time, with admirable judgment, he offered to submit the case to the Supreme Court, and to abide by its decision. By making this proposition he risked nothing; yet it was a proposition which his opponents could hardly reject. Nobody could be treated as a criminal for obeying what the judges should solemnly pronounce to be the lawful govern-

ment. The boldest man would shrink from taking
arms in defence of what the judges should pronounce
to be usurpation. Clavering and Francis, after some
delay, unwillingly consented to abide by the award of
the court. The court pronounced that the resignation 5
was invalid, and that therefore Hastings was still
Governor-General under the Regulating Act; and the
defeated members of the Council, finding that the
sense of the whole settlement was against them,
acquiesced in the decision. 10

About this time arrived the news that, after a suit
which had lasted several years, the Franconian courts
had decreed a divorce between Imhoff and his wife.
The Baron left Calcutta, carrying with him the means
of buying an estate in Saxony. The lady became 15
Mrs. Hastings. The event was celebrated by great
festivities; and all the most conspicuous persons at
Calcutta, without distinction of parties, were invited
to the Government-house. Clavering, as the Mohammedan chronicler tells the story, was sick in mind and 20
body, and excused himself from joining the splendid
assembly. But Hastings, whom, as it should seem,
success in ambition and in love had put into high
good-humor, would take no denial. He went himself
to the General's house, and at length brought his 25

vanquished rival in triumph to the gay circle which surrounded the bride. The exertion was too much for a frame broken by mortification as well as by disease. Clavering died a few days later.

Wheler, who came out expecting to be Governor-General, and was forced to content himself with a seat at the council-board, generally voted with Francis. But the Governor-General, with Barwell's help and his own casting vote, was still the master. Some change took place at this time in the feeling both of the Court of Directors and of the Ministers of the Crown. All designs against Hastings were dropped; and, when his original term of five years expired, he was quietly reappointed. The truth is, that the fearful dangers to which the public interests in every quarter were now exposed, made both Lord North and the Company unwilling to part with a Governor whose talents, experience, and resolution, enmity itself was compelled to acknowledge.

The crisis was indeed formidable. The great and victorious empire, on the throne of which George the Third had taken his seat °eighteen years before, with brighter hopes than had attended the accession of any of the long line of English sovereigns, had, by the most senseless misgovernment, been brought to the

verge of ruin. In America millions of Englishmen
were at war with the country from which their blood,
their language, their religion, and their institutions
were derived, and to which, but a short time before,
they had been as strongly attached as the inhabitants
of Norfolk and Leicestershire. The great powers of
Europe, humbled to the dust by the °vigor and genius
which had guided the councils of George the Second,
now rejoiced in the prospect of a signal revenge. The
time was approaching when our island, while struggling to keep down the United States of America, and
pressed with a still nearer danger by the too just dis-
contents of Ireland, was to be assailed by France,
Spain, and Holland, and to be threatened by the
armed neutrality of the Baltic; when even our maritime supremacy was to be in jeopardy; when hostile
fleets were to command the Straits of °Calpe and the
Mexican Sea; when the British flag was to be scarcely
able to protect the British Channel. Great as were
the faults of Hastings, it was happy for our country
that at that conjuncture, the most terrible through
which she has ever passed, he was the ruler of her
Indian dominions.

An attack by sea on Bengal was little to be apprehended. The danger was that the European enemies

of England might form an alliance with some native
power, might furnish that power with troops, arms,
and ammunition, and might thus assail our possessions on the side of the land.   It was chiefly from the
5 °Mahrattas that Hastings anticipated danger.   The
original seat of that singular people was the wild
range of hills which runs along the western coast of
India.   In the reign of Aurungzebe the inhabitants
of those regions, led by the great Sevajee, began to
10 descend on the possessions of their wea tier and less
warlike neighbors.   The energy, ferocity, and cunning
of the Mahrattas, soon made them the most conspicuous among the new powers which were generated by
the corruption of the decaying monarchy.   At first
15 they were only robbers.   They soon rose to the dignity of conquerors.   Half the provinces of the empire
were turned into Mahratta principalities.   Freebooters,
sprung from low castes, and accustomed to menial
employments, became mighty Rajahs.   The Bonslas,
20 at the head of a band of plunderers, occupied the vast
region of Berar.   The Guicowar, which is, being interpreted, the Herdsmen, founded that dynasty which
still reigns in Guzerat.   The houses of Scindia and
Holkar waxed great in Malwa.   One adventurous cap-
25 tain made his nest on the impregnable rock of Gooti.

Another became the lord of the thousand villages which are scattered among the green rice-fields of Tanjore.

That was the time, throughout India, of double government. The form and the power were every where separated. The Mussulman nabobs who had become sovereign princes, the Vizier in Oude, and the Nizam at Hyderabad, still called themselves the viceroys of the house of Tamerlane. In the same manner the Mahratta states, though really independent of each other, pretended to be members of one empire. They all acknowledged, by words and ceremonies, the supremacy of the heir of Sevajee, a *roi fainéant* who chewed bang and toyed with dancing girls in a state prison at Sattara, and of his Peshwa or mayor of the palace, a great hereditary magistrate, who kept a court with kingly state at Poonah, and whose authority was obeyed in the spacious provinces of Aurungabad and Bejapoor.

Some months before war was declared in Europe the government of Bengal was alarmed by the news that a French adventurer, who passed for a man of quality, had arrived at Poonah. It was said that he had been received there with great distinction, that he had delivered to the Peshwa letters and presents from

G

Lewis the Sixteenth, and that a treaty, hostile to
England, had been concluded between France and the
Mahrattas.

Hastings immediately resolved to strike the first
blow. The title of the Peshwa was not undisputed.
A portion of the Mahratta nation was favorable to
a pretender. The Governor-General determined to
espouse this pretender's interest, to move an army
across the peninsula of India, and to form a close
alliance with the chief of the house of Bonsla, who
ruled Berar, and who, in power and dignity, was
inferior to none of the Mahratta princes.

The army had marched, and the negotiations with
Berar were in progress, when a letter from the English
consul at Cairo brought the news that war had been
proclaimed both in London and Paris. All the measures which the crisis required were adopted by Hastings without a moment's delay. The French factories
in Bengal were seized. Orders were sent to Madras
that Pondicherry should instantly be occupied. Near
Calcutta, works were thrown up which were thought
to render the approach of a hostile force impossible.
A maritime establishment was formed for the defence
of the river. Nine new battalions of sepoys were
raised, and a corps of native artillery was formed out

of the hardy Lascars of the Bay of Bengal. Having
made these arrangements, the Governor-General with
calm confidence pronounced his presidency secure from
all attack, unless the Mahrattas should march against
it in conjunction with the French.

The expedition which Hastings had sent westward
was not so speedily or completely successful as most
of his undertakings. The commanding officer pro-
crastinated. The authorities at Bombay blundered.
But the Governor-General persevered. A new commander repaired the errors of his predecessor. Several
brilliant actions spread the military renown of the
English through regions where no European flag had
ever been seen. It is probable that, if a °new and
more formidable danger had not compelled Hastings
to change his whole policy, his plans respecting the
Mahratta empire would have been carried into complete
effect.

The authorities in England had wisely sent out to
Bengal, as commander of the forces and member of the
Council, one of the most distinguished soldiers of that
time. Sir Eyre Coote had, many years before, been
conspicuous among the founders of the British empire
in the East. At the council of war which preceded
the battle of Plassey, he earnestly recommended, in

opposition to the majority, that daring course which,
after some hesitation, was adopted, and which was
crowned with such splendid success. He subsequently
commanded in the south of India against the brave
5 and unfortunate °Lally, gained the decisive battle of
Wandewash over the French and their native allies,
took Pondicherry, and made the English power supreme
in the Carnatic. Since those great exploits near
twenty years had elapsed. Coote had no longer the
10 bodily activity which he had shown in earlier days;
nor was the vigor of his mind altogether unimpaired.
He was capricious and fretful, and required much
coaxing to keep him in good-humor. It must, we
fear, be added that the love of money had grown upon
15 him, and that he thought more about his allowances,
and less about his duties, than might have been
expected from so eminent a member of so noble a
profession. Still he was perhaps the ablest officer
that was then to be found in the British army. Among
20 the native soldiers his name was great and his influence unrivalled. Nor is he yet forgotten by them.
Now and then a white-bearded old sepoy may still be
found, who loves to talk of °Porto Novo and Pollilore.
It is but a short time since one of those aged men
25 came to present a memorial to an English officer, who

holds one of the highest employments in India. A print of Coote hung in the room. The veteran recognized at once that face and figure which he had not seen for more than half a century, and, forgetting his salam to the living, halted, drew himself up, lifted his hand, and with solemn reverence paid his military obeisance to the dead.

Coote, though he did not, like Barwell, vote constantly with the Governor-General, was by no means inclined to join in systematic opposition, and on most questions concurred with Hastings, who did his best, by assiduous courtship, and by readily granting the most exorbitant allowances, to gratify the strongest passions of the old soldier.

It seemed likely at this time that a general reconciliation would put an end to the quarrels which had, during some years, weakened and disgraced the government of Bengal. The dangers of the empire might well induce men of patriotic feeling, — and of patriotic feeling neither Hastings nor Francis was destitute, — to forget private enmities, and to co-operate heartily for the general good. Coote had never been concerned in faction. Wheler was thoroughly tired of it. Barwell had made an ample fortune, and, though he had promised that he would not leave

Calcutta while his help was needed in Council, was most desirous to return to England, and exerted himself to promote an arrangement which would set him at liberty.

A compact was made, by which Francis agreed to desist from opposition, and Hastings engaged that the friends of Francis should be admitted to a fair share of the honors and emoluments of the service. During a few months after this treaty there was apparent harmony at the council-board.

Harmony, indeed, was never more necessary; for at this moment internal calamities, more formidable than war itself, menaced Bengal. The authors of the Regulating Act of 1773 had established two independent powers, the one judicial, the other political; and, with a carelessness scandalously common in English legislation, had omitted to define the limits of either. The judges took advantage of the indistinctness, and attempted to draw to themselves supreme authority, not only within Calcutta, but through the whole of the great territory subject to the Presidency of Fort William. There are few Englishmen who will not admit that the English law, in spite of modern improvements, is neither so cheap nor so speedy as might be wished. Still, it is a system which has grown up among us. In some points, it has been fashioned to suit our feelings; in others, it has gradually fashioned our feelings to suit itself. Even to its worst evils we are accustomed; and therefore, though we may complain of them, they do not strike us with the horror and dismay which would be produced by a new grievance of smaller severity. In India the case is widely different. English law, transplanted to that country, has all the vices from which we suffer here; it has them all in a far higher degree; and it has other vices, compared with which the worst vices from which we suffer are trifles. Dilatory here, it is far more dilatory in a land where the help of an interpreter is needed by every judge and by every advocate. Costly here, it is far more costly in a land into which the legal practitioners must be imported from an immense distance. All English labor in India, from the labor of the Governor-General and the Commander-in-Chief, down to that of a groom or a watchmaker, must be paid for at a higher rate than at home. No man will be banished, and banished to the torrid zone, for nothing. The rule holds good with respect to the legal profession. No English barrister will work, fifteen thousand miles from all his friends, with the thermometer at ninety-six in the shade, for the emolu-

ments which will content him in °chambers that
overlook the Thames. Accordingly, the fees at Calcutta are about three times as great as the fees of
Westminster Hall; and this, though the people of
5 India are, beyond all comparison, poorer than the
people of England.' Yet the delay and the expense,
grievous as they are, form the smallest part of the
evil which English law, °imported without modifications into India, could not fail to produce. The
10 strongest feelings of our nature, honor, religion, female
modesty, rose up against the innovation. Arrest on
mesne process was the first step in most civil proceedings; and to a native of rank arrest was not
merely a restraint, but a foul personal indignity.
15 Oaths were required in every stage of every suit;
and the feeling of a Quaker about an oath is hardly
stronger than that of a respectable native. That the
apartments of a woman of quality should be entered
by strange men, or that her face should be seen by
20 them, are, in the East, intolerable outrages, outrages
which are more dreaded than death, and which can be
expiated only by the shedding of blood. To these
outrages the most distinguished families of Bengal,
Bahar, and Orissa, were now exposed. Imagine what
25 the state of our own country would be, if a jurispru-

dence were on a sudden introduced among us, which should be to us what our jurisprudence was to our Asiatic subjects. Imagine what the state of our country would be, if it were enacted that any man, by merely swearing that a debt was due to him, should acquire a right to insult the persons of men of the most honorable and sacred callings and of women of the most shrinking delicacy, to horsewhip a general officer, to put a bishop in the stocks, to treat ladies in the way which called forth the blow of Wat Tyler. Something like this was the effect of the attempt which the Supreme Court made to extend its jurisdiction over the whole of the °Company's territory.

A reign of terror began, of terror heightened by mystery; for even that which was endured was less horrible than that which was anticipated. No man knew what was next to be expected from this strange tribunal. It came from beyond the black water, as the people of India, with mysterious horror, call the sea. It consisted of judges not one of whom was familiar with the usages of the millions over whom they claimed boundless authority. Its records were kept in unknown characters; its sentences were pronounced in unknown sounds. It had already collected round itself an army of the worst part of the native

population, informers, and false witnesses, and common barrators, and agents of chicane, and above all,
a banditti of bailiffs' followers, compared with whom
the retainers of the worst English spunging-houses, in
the worst times, might be considered as upright and
tender-hearted.   Many natives, highly considered
among their countrymen, were seized, hurried up to
Calcutta, flung into the common gaol, not for any
crime even imputed, not for any debt that had been
proved, but merely as a precaution till their cause
should come to trial.   There were instances in which
men of the most venerable dignity, persecuted without
a cause by extortioners, died of rage and shame in the
grip of the vile °alguazils of Impey. The harems of
noble Mahommedans, sanctuaries respected in the
East by governments which respected nothing else,
were burst open by gangs of bailiffs. The Mussulmans, braver and less accustomed to submission than
the Hindoos, sometimes stood on their defence; and
there were instances in which they shed their blood in
the doorway, while defending, sword in hand, the
sacred apartments of their women. Nay, it seemed
as if even the faint-hearted Bengalee, who had
crouched at the feet of Surajah Dowlah, who had been
mute during the administration of Vansittart, would

at length find courage in despair. No Mahratta invasion had ever spread through the province such dismay as this inroad of English lawyers. All the
injustice of former oppressors, Asiatic and European,
appeared as a blessing when compared with the justice 5
of the Supreme Court.

Every class of the population, English and native,
with the exception of the ravenous pettifoggers who
fattened on the misery and terror of an immense com-
munity, cried out loudly against this fearful oppres- 10
sion. But the judges were immovable. If a bailiff
was resisted, they ordered the soldiers to be called
out. If a servant of the Company, in conformity
with the orders of the government, withstood the
miserable catchpoles who, with Impey's writs in their 15
hands, exceeded the insolence and rapacity of gang-
robbers, he was flung into prison for a contempt. The
lapse of sixty years, the virtue and wisdom of many
eminent magistrates who have during that time administered justice in the Supreme Court, have not 20
effaced from the minds of the people of Bengal the
recollection of those evil days.

The members of the government were, on this subject, united as one man. Hastings had courted the
judges, he had found them useful instruments; but 25

he was not disposed to make them his own masters, or the masters of India. His mind was large; his knowledge of the native character most accurate. He saw that the system pursued by the Supreme Court was degrading to the government and ruinous to the people; and he resolved to oppose it manfully. The consequence was, that the friendship, if that be the proper word for such a connection, which had existed between him and Impey, was for a time completely dissolved. The government placed itself firmly between the tyrannical tribunal and the people. The Chief Justice proceeded to the wildest excesses. The Governor-General and all the members of Council were served with writs, calling on them to appear before the King's justices, and to answer for their public acts. This was too much. Hastings, with just scorn, refused to obey the call, set at liberty the persons wrongfully detained by the Court, and took measures for resisting the outrageous proceedings of the sheriffs' officers, if necessary, by the sword. But he had in view another device which might prevent the necessity of an appeal to arms. He was seldom at a loss for an expedient; and he knew Impey well. The expedient, in this case, was a very simple one, neither more nor less than a bribe.

Impey was, by act of Parliament, a judge, independent of the government of Bengal, and entitled to a salary of eight thousand a year. Hastings proposed to make him also a judge in the Company's service, removable at the pleasure of the government of Bengal; and to give him, in that capacity, about eight thousand a year more. It was understood that, in consideration of this new salary, Impey would desist from urging the high pretensions of his court. If he did urge these pretensions, the government could, at a moment's notice, eject him from the new place which had been created for him. The bargain was struck; Bengal was saved; an appeal to force was averted; and the Chief Justice was °rich, quiet, and infamous.

Of Impey's conduct it is unnecessary to speak. It was of a piece with almost every part of his conduct that comes under the notice of history. No other such judge has dishonored the English ermine, since Jeffreys drank himself to death in the Tower. But we cannot agree with those who have blamed Hastings for this transaction. The case stood thus. The negligent manner in which the Regulating Act had been framed put it in the power of the Chief Justice to throw a great country into the most dreadful confusion.

He was determined to use his power to the utmost, unless he was paid to be still; and Hastings consented to pay him. The necessity was to be deplored. It is also to be deplored that pirates should be able to exact ransom, by threatening to make their captives walk the plank. But to ransom a captive from pirates has always been held a humane and Christian act; and it would be absurd to charge the payer of the ransom with corrupting the virtue of the corsair. This, we seriously think, is a not unfair illustration of the relative position of Impey, Hastings, and the people of India. Whether it was right in Impey to demand or to accept a price for powers which, if they really belonged to him, he could not abdicate, which, if they did not belong to him, he ought never to have usurped, and which in neither case he could honestly sell, is one question. It is quite another question, whether Hastings was not right to give any sum, however large, to any man, however worthless, rather than either surrender millions of human beings to pillage, or rescue them by civil war.

Francis strongly opposed this arrangement. It may, indeed, be suspected that personal aversion to Impey was as strong a motive with Francis as regard for the welfare of the province. To a mind burning with

resentment, it might seem better to leave Bengal to
the oppressors than to redeem it by enriching them.
It is not improbable, on the other hand, that Hastings
may have been the more willing to resort to an expedient agreeable to the Chief Justice, because that
high functionary had already been so serviceable, and
might, when existing dissensions were composed, be
serviceable again.

But it was not on this point alone that Francis was
now opposed to Hastings. The peace between them
proved to be only a short and hollow truce, during
which their mutual aversion was constantly becoming
stronger. At length an explosion took place. Hastings publicly charged Francis with having deceived
him, and with having induced Barwell to quit the
service by insincere promises. Then came a dispute,
such as frequently arises even between honorable men
when they may make important agreements by mere
verbal communication. An impartial historian will
probably be of opinion that they had misunderstood
each other; but their minds were so much embittered
that they imputed to each other nothing less than deliberate villany. "I do not," said Hastings, in a minute
recorded on the Consultations of the Government, "I
do not trust to Mr. Francis's promises of candor, con-

vinced that he is incapable of it. I judge of his public
conduct by his private, which I have found to be void
of truth and honor." After the Council had risen,
Francis put a challenge into the Governor-General's
5 hand. It was instantly accepted. They met, and
fired. Francis was shot through the body. He was
carried to a neighboring house, where it appeared that
the wound, though severe, was not mortal. Hastings
inquired repeatedly after his enemy's health, and pro-
10 posed to call on him; but Francis coldly declined
the visit. He had a proper sense, he said, of the
Governor General's politeness, but could not consent
to any private interview. They could meet only at
the council-board.

In a very short time it was made signally manifest
to how great a danger the Governor-General had, on
this occasion, exposed his country. A crisis arrived
with which he, and he alone, was competent to deal.
It is not too much to say that, if he had been taken
20 from the head of affairs, the years 1780 and 1781
would have been as fatal to our power in Asia as to
our power in America.

The Mahrattas had been the chief objects of apprehension to Hastings. The measures which he had
25 adopted for the purpose of breaking their power, had

at first been frustrated by the errors of those whom
he was compelled to employ; but his perseverance
and ability seemed likely to be crowned with success,
when a far more formidable danger showed itself in a
distant quarter. 5

°About thirty years before this time, a Mahommedan
soldier had begun to distinguish himself in the wars
of Southern India. His education had been neglected;
his extraction was humble. His father had been a
petty officer of revenue; his grandfather a wandering 10
dervise. But though thus meanly descended, though
ignorant even of the alphabet, the adventurer had no
sooner been placed at the head of a body of troops
than he approved himself a man born for conquest
and command. Among the crowd of chiefs who were 15
struggling for a share of India, none could compare
with him in the qualities of the captain and the statesman. He became a general; he became a sovereign.
Out of the fragments of old principalities, which had
gone to pieces in the general wreck, he formed for 20
himself a great, compact, and vigorous empire. That
empire he ruled with the ability, severity, and vigi-
lance of Lewis the Eleventh. Licentious in his pleasures, implacable in his revenge, he had yet enlargement
of mind enough to perceive how much the prosperity 25

H

of subjects adds to the strength of governments. He
was an oppressor; but he had at least the merit of
protecting his people against all oppression except his
own. He was now in extreme old age; but his intellect
5 was as clear, and his spirit as high, as in the prime
of manhood. Such was the great °Hyder Ali, the
founder of the Mahommedan kingdom of Mysore, and
the most formidable enemy with whom the English
conquerors of India have ever had to contend.

10   Had Hastings been governor of Madras, Hyder
would have been either made a friend, or vigorously
encountered as an enemy. Unhappily the English
authorities in the south provoked their powerful
neighbor's hostility, without being prepared to repel
15 it. On a sudden, an army of ninety thousand men,
far superior in discipline and efficiency to any other
native force that could be found in India, came pouring through those wild passes which, worn by mountain torrents, and dark with jungle, lead down from
20 the table-land of Mysore to the plains of the Carnatic.
This great army was accompanied by a hundred pieces
of cannon; and its movements were guided by many
French officers, trained in the best military schools of
Europe.

25   Hyder was everywhere triumphant. The sepoys in

many British garrisons flung down their arms. Some forts were surrendered by treachery and some by despair. In a few days the whole open country north of the Coleroon had submitted. The English inhabitants of Madras could already see by night, from the top of Mount St. Thomas, the western sky reddened by a vast semicircle of blazing villages. The white villas, to which our countrymen retire after the daily labors of government and of trade, when the cool evening breeze springs up from the bay, were now left without inhabitants; for bands of the fierce horsemen of Mysore had already been seen prowling among the tulip-trees and near the gay verandas. Even the town was not thought secure, and the British merchants and public functionaries made haste to crowd themselves behind the cannon of Fort St. George.

There were the means, indeed, of assembling an army which might have defended the presidency, and even driven the invader back to his mountains. Sir Hector Munro was at the head of one considerable force; Baillie was advancing with another. United, they might have presented a formidable front even to such an enemy as Hyder. But the English commanders, neglecting those fundamental rules of the military art of which the propriety is obvious even to

men who have never received a military education,
deferred their junction, and were separately attacked.
Baillie's detachment was destroyed.   Munro was forced
to abandon his baggage, to °fling his guns into the tanks,
and to save himself by a retreat which might be called
a flight.   In three weeks from the commencement of
the war, the British empire in Southern India had been
brought to the verge of ruin.   Only a few fortified
places remained to us.   The glory of our arms had
departed.   It was known that a great French expedition might soon be expected on the coast of Coromandel.
England, beset by enemies on every side, was in no
condition to protect such remote dependencies.

Then it was that the fertile genius and serene courage of Hastings achieved their most signal triumph.
A swift ship, flying before the south-west monsoon,
brought the evil tidings in few days to Calcutta.   In
twenty-four hours the Governor-General had framed
a complete plan of policy adapted to the altered state
of affairs.   The struggle with Hyder was a struggle
for life and death.   All minor objects must be sacri-
ficed to the preservation of the Carnatic.   The disputes
with the Mahrattas must be accommodated.   A large
military force and a supply of money must be instantly
sent to Madras.   But even these measures would be

insufficient, unless the war, hitherto so grossly mismanaged, were placed under the direction of a vigorous mind. It was no time for trifling. Hastings determined to resort to an extreme exercise of power, to suspend the incapable governor of Fort St. George, to send Sir Eyre Coote to oppose Hyder, and to intrust that distinguished general with the whole administration of the war.

In spite of the sullen opposition of Francis, who had now recovered from his wound, and had returned to the Council, the Governor-General's wise and firm policy was approved by the majority of the board. The reinforcements were sent off with great expedition, and reached Madras before the French armament arrived in the Indian seas. Coote, broken by age and disease, was no longer the Coote of Wandewash; but he was still a resolute and skilful commander. The progress of Hyder was arrested; and in a few months the great victory of Porto Novo retrieved the honor of the English arms.

In the mean time Francis had returned to England, and Hastings was now left perfectly unfettered. Wheler had gradually been relaxing in his opposition, and, after the departure of his vehement and implacable colleague, co-operated heartily with the

Governor-General, whose influence over the British in India, always great, had, by the vigor and success of his recent measures, been considerably increased.

But, though the difficulties arising from factions within the Council were at an end, another class of difficulties had become more pressing than ever. The financial embarrassment was extreme. Hastings had to find the means, not only of carrying on the government of Bengal, but of maintaining a most costly war against both Indian and European enemies in the Carnatic, and of making remittances to England. A few years before this time he had obtained relief by plundering the Mogul and enslaving the Rohillas; nor were the resources of his fruitful mind by any means exhausted.

His first design was on °Benares, a city which in wealth, population, dignity, and sanctity, was among the foremost of Asia. It was commonly believed that half a million of human beings was crowded into that labyrinth of lofty alleys, rich with shrines, and minarets, and balconies, and carved oriels, to which the sacred apes clung by hundreds. The traveller could scarcely make his way through the press of holy mendicants and not less holy bulls. The broad and stately flights of steps which descended from these swarming haunts to the bathing-places along the Ganges were worn every day by the footsteps of an innumerable multitude of worshippers. The schools and temples drew crowds of pious Hindoos from every province where the Brahminical faith was known. Hundreds of devotees came thither every month to die: for it was believed that a peculiarly happy fate awaited the man who should pass from the sacred city into the sacred river. Nor was superstition the only motive which allured strangers to that great metropolis. Commerce had as many pilgrims as religion. All along the shores of the venerable stream lay great fleets of vessels laden with rich merchandise. From the looms of Benares went forth the most delicate silks that adorned the balls of St. James's and of Versailles; and in the bazaars the muslins of Bengal and the sabres of Oude were mingled with the jewels of Golconda and the shawls of Cashmere. This rich capital, and the surrounding tract, had long been under the immediate rule of a Hindoo prince, who rendered homage to the Mogul emperors. During the great anarchy of India, the °lords of Benares became independent of the court of Delhi, but were compelled to submit to the authority of the Nabob of Oude. Oppressed by this formidable neighbor, they invoked the

protection of the English. The English protection was
given; and at length the Nabob Vizier, by a solemn
treaty, ceded all his rights over Benares to the Company. From that time the Rajah was the vassal of
the government of Bengal, acknowledged its supremacy, and engaged to send an annual tribute to Fort
William. This tribute Cheyte Sing, the reigning
prince, had paid with strict punctuality.

About the precise nature of the legal relation between the Company and the Rajah of Benares, there
has been much warm and acute controversy. On
the one side, it has been maintained that Cheyte Sing
was merely a great subject on whom the superior
power had a right to call for aid in the necessities of
the empire. On the other side, it has been contended
that he was an independent prince, that the only claim
which the Company had upon him was for a fixed
tribute, and that, while the fixed tribute was regularly
paid, as it assuredly was, the English had no more
right to exact any further contribution from him than
to demand subsidies from Holland or Denmark. Nothing is easier than to find precedents and analogies in
favor of either view.

Our own impression is that neither view is correct.
It was too much the habit of English politicians to

take it for granted that there was in India a known
and definite constitution by which questions of this
kind were to be decided. The truth is that, during
the interval which elapsed between the °fall of the
house of Tamerlane and the establishment of the
British ascendency, there was no such constitution.
The old order of things had passed away; the new
order of things was not yet formed. All was transi-
tion, confusion, obscurity. Every body kept his head
as he best might, and scrambled for whatever he
could get. There have been similar seasons in Europe.
The time of the dissolution of the Carlovingian empire
is an instance. Who would think of seriously discussing the question, what extent of pecuniary aid
and of obedience Hugh Capet had a constitutional
right to demand from the Duke of Britanny or the
Duke of Normandy? The words "constitutional
right" had, in that state of society, no meaning. If
Hugh Capet laid hands on all the possessions of the
Duke of Normandy, this might be unjust and im-
moral; but it would not be illegal, in the sense in
which the ordinances of Charles the Tenth were illegal.
If, on the other hand, the Duke of Normandy made
war on Hugh Capet, this might be unjust and im-
moral; but it would not be illegal, in the sense in

which the expedition of Prince Louis Bonaparte was illegal.

Very similar to this the state of India sixty years ago. Of the existing governments not a single one could lay claim to legitimacy, or could plead any other title than recent occupation. There was scarcely a province in which the real sovereignty and the nominal sovereignty were not disjoined. Titles and forms were still retained which implied that the heir of Tamerlane was an absolute ruler, and that the Nabobs of the provinces were his lieutenants. In reality, he was a captive. The Nabobs were in some places independent princes. In other places, as in Bengal and the Carnatic, they had, like their master, become mere phantoms, and the Company was supreme. Among the Mahrattas, again, the heir of Sevajee still kept the title of Rajah; but he was a prisoner, and his prime minister, the Peshwa, had become the hereditary chief of the state. The Peshwa, in his turn, was fast sinking into the same degraded situation to which he had reduced the Rajah. It was, we believe, impossible to find, from the Himalayas to Mysore, a single government which was at once a government *de facto* and a government *de jure*, which possessed the physical means of making itself feared by its neighbors and subjects, and which had at the same time the authority derived from law and long prescription.

Hastings clearly discerned, what was hidden from most of his contemporaries, that such a state of things gave immense advantages to a ruler of great talents and few scruples. In every international question that could arise, he had his option between the *de facto* ground and the *de jure* ground; and the probability was that one of those grounds would sustain any claim that it might be convenient for him to make, and enable him to resist any claim made by others. In every controversy, accordingly, he resorted to the plea which suited his immediate purpose, without troubling himself in the least about consistency; and thus he scarcely ever failed to find what, to persons of short memories and scanty information, seemed to be a justification for what he wanted to do. Sometimes the Nabob of Bengal is a shadow, sometimes a monarch. Sometimes the Vizier is a mere deputy, sometimes an independent potentate. If it is expedient for the Company to show some legal title to the revenues of Bengal, the grant under the seal of the Mogul is brought forward as an instrument of the highest authority. When the Mogul asks for the rents which were reserved to him by that very grant, he is told that he is a mere pageant, that the English power rests on a very different foundation from a charter given by him, that he is welcome to play at 5 royalty as long as he likes, but that he must expect no tribute from the real masters of India.

It is true that it was in the power of others, as well as of Hastings, to practise this legerdemain; but in the controversies of governments, sophistry is of 10 little use unless it be backed by power. There is a principle which Hastings was fond of asserting in the strongest terms, and on which he acted with undeviating steadiness. It is a principle which, we must own, though it may be grossly abused, can hardly be 15 disputed in the present state of public law. It is this, that where an ambiguous question arises between two governments, there is, if they cannot agree, no appeal except to force, and that the opinion of the stronger must prevail. °Almost every question was ambiguous 20 in India. The English government was the strongest in India. The consequences are obvious. The English government might do exactly what it chose.

The English government now chose to wring money out of Cheyte Sing. It had formerly been convenient 25 to treat him as a sovereign prince; it was now con-

venient to treat him as a subject. Dexterity inferior
to that of Hastings could easily find, in the general
chaos of laws and customs, arguments for either course.
Hastings wanted a great supply. It was known that
Cheyte Sing had a large revenue, and it was suspected
that he had accumulated a treasure. Nor was he a
favorite at Calcutta. He had, when the Governor-General
was in great difficulties, courted the favor of Francis and Clavering. Hastings who, less perhaps from
evil passions than from policy, seldom left an injury
unpunished, was not sorry that the fate of Cheyte
Sing should teach neighboring princes the same lesson
which the fate of Nuncomar had already impressed on
the inhabitants of Bengal.

In 1778, on the first breaking out of the war with
France, Cheyte Sing was called upon to pay, in addition to his fixed tribute, an extraordinary contribution
of fifty thousand pounds. In 1779, an equal sum was
exacted. In 1780, the demand was renewed. Cheyte
Sing, in the hope of obtaining some indulgence, secretly
offered the Governor-General a bribe of twenty thousand pounds. Hastings took the money, and his enemies have maintained that he took it intending to keep
it. He certainly concealed the transaction, for a time,
both from the Council in Bengal and from the Direc-

tors at home; nor did he ever give any satisfactory
reason for the concealment. Public spirit, or the fear
of detection, at last determined him to withstand the
temptation. He paid over the bribe to the Company's
5 treasury, and insisted that the Rajah should instantly
comply with the demands of the English government.
The Rajah, after the fashion of his countrymen, shuf-
fled, solicited, and pleaded poverty. The grasp of
Hastings was not to be so eluded. He added to the
10 requisition another ten thousand pounds as a fine for
delay, and sent troops to exact the money.

The money was paid. But this was not enough.
The late events in the south of India had increased
the financial embarrassments of the Company. Hast-
15 ings was determined to plunder Cheyte Sing, and, for
that end, to fasten a quarrel on him. Accordingly, the
Rajah was now required to keep a body of cavalry for
the service of the British government. He objected
and evaded. This was exactly what the Governor-
20 General wanted. He had now a pretext for treating
the wealthiest of his vassals as a criminal. "I resolved," — these are the words of Hastings himself,
— "to draw from his guilt the means of relief of the
Company's distresses, to make him pay largely for
25 his pardon, or to exact a severe vengeance for past

delinquency." The plan was simply this, to demand larger and larger contributions till the Rajah should be driven to remonstrate, then to call his remonstrance a crime, and to punish him by confiscating all his possessions.

Cheyte Sing was in the greatest dismay. He offered two hundred thousand pounds to propitiate the British government. But Hastings replied that nothing less than half a million would be accepted. Nay, he began to think of selling Benares to Oude, as he had formerly sold Allahabad and Rohilcund. The matter was one which could not be well managed at a distance; and Hastings resolved to visit Benares.

Cheyte Sing received his liege lord with every mark of reverence, came near sixty miles, with his guards, to meet and escort the illustrious visitor, and expressed his deep concern at the displeasure of the English. He even took off his turban, and laid it in the lap of Hastings, a gesture which in India marks the most profound submission and devotion. Hastings behaved with cold and repulsive severity. Having arrived at Benares, he sent to the Rajah a paper containing the demands of the government of Bengal. The Rajah, in reply, attempted to clear himself from the accusations brought against him. Hastings, who

wanted money and not excuses, was not to be put off
by the ordinary artifices of Eastern negotiation.   He
instantly ordered the Rajah to be arrested and placed
under the custody of two companies of sepoys.

5   In taking these strong measures, Hastings scarcely
showed his usual judgment.   It is possible that, having had little opportunity of personally observing any
part of the population of India, except the Bengalees,
he was not fully aware of the difference between their
10 character and that of the tribes which inhabit the
upper provinces.   He was now in a land far more
favorable to the vigor of the human frame than the
Delta of the Ganges; in a land fruitful of soldiers, who
have been found worthy to follow English battalions to
15 the charge and into the breach.   The Rajah was popular among his subjects.   His administration had been
mild; and the prosperity of the district which he
governed presented a striking contrast to the depressed
state of Bahar under our rule, and a still more strik-
20 ing contrast to the misery of the provinces which
were cursed by the tyranny of the Nabob Vizier.   The
national and religious prejudices with which the English were regarded throughout India were peculiarly
intense in the metropolis of the Brahminical supersti-
25 tion.   It can therefore scarcely be doubted that the

Governor-General, before he outraged the dignity of Cheyte Sing by an arrest, ought to have assembled a force capable of bearing down all opposition. This had not been done. The handful of sepoys who attended Hastings would probably have been sufficient to overawe Moorshedabad, or the Black Town of Calcutta. But they were unequal to a conflict with the hardy rabble of Benares. The streets surrounding the palace were filled with an immense multitude, of whom a large proportion, as is usual in Upper India, wore arms. The tumult became a fight, and the fight a massacre. The English officers defended themselves with desperate courage against overwhelming numbers, and fell, as became them, sword in hand. The sepoys were butchered. The gates were forced. The captive prince, neglected by his jailers during the confusion, discovered an outlet which opened on the precipitous bank of the Ganges, let himself down to the water by a string made of the turbans of his attendants, found a boat, and escaped to the opposite shore.

If Hastings had, by indiscreet violence, brought himself into a difficult and perilous situation, it is only just to acknowledge that he extricated himself with even more than his usual ability and presence of mind. He had only fifty men with him. The building in

which he had taken up his residence was on every
side blockaded by the insurgents. But his fortitude
remained unshaken. The Rajah from the other side
of the river sent apologies and liberal offers. They
were not even answered. Some subtle and enterpris-
ing men were found who undertook to pass through
the throng of enemies, and to convey the intelligence
of the late events to the English cantonments. It is the
fashion of the natives of India to wear large earrings
of gold. When they travel, the rings are laid aside,
lest the precious metal should tempt some gang of
robbers; and, in place of the ring, a quill or a roll
of paper is inserted in the orifice to prevent it from
closing. Hastings placed in the ears of his messengers
letters rolled up in the smallest compass. Some of
these letters were addressed to the commanders of the
English troops. One was written to assure his wife
of his safety. One was to the envoy whom he had
sent to negotiate with the Mahrattas. Instructions
for the negotiation were needed; and the Governor-
General framed them in that situation of extreme
danger, with as much composure as if he had been
writing in his palace at Calcutta.

Things, however, were not yet at the worst. An
English officer of more spirit than judgment, eager to

distinguish himself, made a premature attack on the insurgents beyond the river. His troops were entangled in narrow streets, and assailed by a furious population. He fell, with many of his men; and the survivors were forced to retire. 5

This event produced the effect which has never failed to follow every check, however slight, sustained in India by the English arms. For hundreds of miles round, the whole country was in commotion. The entire population of the district of Benares took 10 arms. The fields were abandoned by the husbandmen, who thronged to defend their prince. The infection spread to Oude. The oppressed people of that province rose up against the Nabob Vizier, refused to pay their imposts, and put the revenue officers to 15 flight. Even Bahar was ripe for revolt. The hopes of Cheyte Sing began to rise. Instead of imploring mercy in the humble style of a vassal, he began to talk the language of a conqueror, and threatened, it was said, to sweep the white usurpers out of the land. 20 But the English troops were now assembling fast. The officers, and even the private men, regarded the Governor-General with enthusiastic attachment, and flew to his aid with an alacrity which, as he boasted, had never been shown on any other occasion. Major Pop- 25 ham, a brave and skilful soldier, who had highly distinguished himself in the Mahratta war, and in whom the Governor-General reposed the greatest confidence, took the command. The tumultuary army of the Rajah was put to rout. His fastnesses were stormed. In a few hours, above thirty thousand men left his standard, and returned to their ordinary avocations. The unhappy prince fled from his country for ever. His fair domain was added to the British dominions. One of his relations indeed was appointed rajah; but the Rajah of Benares was henceforth to be, like the Nabob of Bengal, a mere pensioner.

By this revolution, an addition of two hundred thousand pounds a year was made to the revenues of the Company. But the immediate relief was not as great as had been expected. The treasure laid up by Cheyte Sing had been popularly estimated at a million sterling. It turned out to be about a fourth part of that sum; and, such as it was, it was seized by the army, and divided as prize-money.

Disappointed in his expectations from Benares, Hastings was more violent than he would otherwise have been, in his dealings with Oude. Sujah Dowlah had long been dead. His son and successor, Asaph-ul-Dowlah, was one of the weakest and most vicious even of Eastern princes. His life was divided between torpid repose and the most odious forms of sensuality. In his court there was boundless waste, throughout his dominions wretchedness and disorder. He had been, under the skilful management of the English government, gradually sinking from the rank of an independent prince to that of a vassal of the Company. It was only by the help of a British brigade that he could be secure from the aggressions of neighbors who despised his weakness, and from the vengeance of subjects who detested his tyranny. A brigade was furnished; and he engaged to defray the charge of paying and maintaining it. From that time his independence was at an end. Hastings was not a man to lose the advantage which he had thus gained. The Nabob soon began to complain of the burden which he had undertaken to bear. His revenues, he said, were falling off; his servants were unpaid; he could no longer support the expense of the arrangement which he had sanctioned. Hastings would not listen to these representations. The Vizier, he said, had invited the government of Bengal to send him troops and had promised to pay for them. The troops had been sent. How long the troops were to remain in Oude was a matter not settled by the treaty. It remained, there-

fore, to be settled between the contracting parties.
But the contracting parties differed. Who then must
decide? The stronger.

Hastings also argued that, if the English force was
withdrawn, Oude would certainly become a prey to
anarchy, and would probably be overrun by a Mahratta army. That the finances of Oude were embarrassed he admitted. But he contended, not without
reason, that the embarrassment was to be attributed
to the incapacity and vices of Asaph-ul-Dowlah himself, and that, if less were spent on the troops, the
only effect would be that more would be squandered
on worthless favorites.

Hastings had intended, after settling the affairs of
Benares, to visit Lucknow, and there to confer with
Asaph-ul-Dowlah. But the obsequious courtesy of
the Nabob Vizier prevented this visit. With a small
train he hastened to meet the Governor-General. An
interview took place in the fortress which, from the
crest of the precipitous rock of Chunar, looks down
on the waters of the Ganges.

At first sight it might appear impossible that the
negotiations should come to an amicable close. Hastings wanted an extraordinary supply of money.
Asaph-ul-Dowlah wanted to obtain a remission of

what he already owed. Such a difference seemed to admit of no compromise. There was, however, one course satisfactory to both sides, one course by which it was possible to relieve the finances both of Oude and of Bengal; and that course was adopted. It was simply this, that the Governor-General and the Nabob Vizier should join to rob a third party; and the third party whom they determined to rob was the parent of one of the robbers.

The mother of the late Nabob, and his wife, who was the mother of the present Nabob, were known as the Begums or Princesses of Oude. They had possessed great influence over Sujah Dowlah, and had, at his death, been left in possession of a splendid °dotation. The domains of which they received the rents and administered the government were of wide extent. The treasure hoarded by the late Nabob, a treasure which was popularly estimated at near three millions sterling, was in their hands. They continued to occupy his favorite palace at Fyzabad, the Beautiful Dwelling; while Asaph-ul-Dowlah held his court in the stately Lucknow, which he had built for himself on the shores of the Goomti, and had adorned with noble mosques and colleges.

Asaph-ul-Dowlah had already extorted considerable

sums from his mother. She had at length appealed to the English; and the English had interfered. A solemn compact had been made, by which she consented to give her son some pecuniary assistance, and he in his turn promised never to commit any further invasion of her rights. This compact was formally guaranteed by the government of Bengal. But times had changed; money was wanted; and the power which had given the guarantee was not ashamed to instigate the spoiler to excesses such that even he shrank from them.

It was necessary to find some pretext for a confiscation inconsistent, not merely with plighted faith, not merely with the ordinary rules of humanity and justice, but also with that great law of filial piety which, even in the wildest tribes of savages, even in those more degraded communities which wither under the influence of a corrupt half-civilization, retains a certain authority over the human mind. A pretext was the last thing that Hastings was likely to want. The insurrection at Benares had produced disturbances in Oude. These disturbances it was convenient to impute to the Princesses. Evidence for the imputation there was scarcely any; unless reports wandering from one mouth to another, and gaining something by every transmission, may be called evidence. The accused were furnished with no charge; they were permitted to make no defence; for the Governor-General wisely considered that, if he tried them, he might not be able to find a ground for plundering them. It was agreed between him and the Nabob Vizier that the noble ladies should, by a sweeping act of confiscation, be stripped of their domains and treasures for the benefit of the Company, and that the sums thus obtained should be accepted by the government of Bengal in satisfaction of its claims on the government of Oude.

While Asaph-ul-Dowlah was at Chunar, he was completely subjugated by the clear and commanding intellect of the English statesman. But, when they had separated, the Vizier began to reflect with uneasiness on the engagements into which he had entered. His mother and grandmother protested and implored. His heart, deeply corrupted by absolute power and licentious pleasures, yet not naturally unfeeling, failed him in this crisis. Even the English resident at Lucknow, though hitherto devoted to Hastings, shrank from extreme measures. But the Governor-General was inexorable. He wrote to the resident in terms of the greatest severity, and declared that, if the

spoliation which had been agreed upon were not instantly carried into effect, he would himself go to Lucknow, and do that from which feebler minds recoil with dismay. The resident, thus menaced, waited
5 on his Highness, and insisted that the treaty of Chunar should be carried into full and immediate effect. Asaph-ul-Dowlah yielded, making at the same time a solemn protestation that he yielded to compulsion. The lands were resumed; but the treasure
10 was not so easily obtained. It was necessary to use violence. A body of the Company's troops marched to Fyzabad, and forced the gates of the palace. The Princesses were confined to their own apartments. But still they refused to submit. Some more stringent
15 mode of coercion was to be found. A mode was found of which, even at this distance of time, we cannot speak without shame and sorrow.

There were at Fyzabad two ancient men, belonging to that unhappy class which a practice, of immemorial
20 antiquity in the East, has excluded from the pleasures of love and from the hope of posterity. It has always been held in Asiatic courts that beings thus estranged from sympathy with their kind are those whom princes may most safely trust. Sujah Dowlah had been of
25 this opinion. He had given his entire confidence to

the two eunuchs; and after his death they remained
at the head of the household of his widow.

These men were, by the orders of the British government, seized, imprisoned, ironed, starved almost to
death, in order to extort money from the Princesses. 5
After they had been two months in confinement,
their health gave way. They implored permission to
take a little exercise in the garden of their prison.
The officer who was in charge of them stated that, if
they were allowed this indulgence, there was not the 10
smallest chance of their escaping, and that their irons
really added nothing to the security of the custody in
which they were kept. He did not understand the
plan of his superiors. Their object in these inflictions
was not security, but torture; and all mitigation was 15
refused. Yet this was not the worst. It was resolved
by an English government that these two infirm old
men should be delivered to the tormentors. For that
purpose they were removed to Lucknow. What
horrors their dungeon there witnessed can only be 20
guessed. But there remains on the records of Parliament, this letter, written by a British resident to a
British soldier.

"Sir, The Nabob having determined to inflict cor-
poral punishment upon the prisoners under your 25

guard, this is to desire that his officers, when they shall come, may have free access to the prisoners, and be permitted to do with them as they shall see proper."

5 While these barbarities were perpetrated at Lucknow, the Princesses were still under duress at Fyzabad. Food was allowed to enter their apartments only in such scanty quantities that their female attendants were in danger of perishing with hunger. Month after 10 month this cruelty continued, till at length, after twelve hundred thousand pounds had been wrung out of the Princesses, Hastings began to think that he had really got to the bottom of their coffers, and that no rigor could extort more. Then at length the 15 wretched men who were detained at Lucknow regained their liberty. When their irons were knocked off, and the doors of their prisons opened, their quivering lips, the tears which ran down their cheeks, and the thanksgivings which they poured forth to the com-20 mon Father of Mussulmans and Christians, melted even the stout hearts of the English warriors who stood by.

But we must not forget to do justice to Sir Elijah Impey's conduct on this occasion. It was not indeed 25 easy for him to intrude himself into a business so entirely alien from all his official duties. But there was something inexpressibly alluring, we must suppose, in the peculiar rankness of the infamy which was then to be got at Lucknow. He hurried thither as fast as relays of palanquin-bearers could carry him. A crowd of people came before him with affidavits against the Begums, ready drawn in their hands. Those affidavits he did not read. Some of them, indeed, he could not read; for they were in the dialects of Northern India, and no interpreter was employed. He administered the oath to the deponents with all possible expedition, and asked not a single question, not even whether they had perused the statements to which they swore. This work performed, he got again into his palanquin, and posted back to Calcutta, to be in time for the opening of term. The cause was one which, by his own confession, lay altogether out of his jurisdiction. Under the charter of justice, he had no more right to inquire into crimes committed by Asiatics in Oude than the Lord President of the Court of Session of Scotland to hold an assize at Exeter. He had no right to try the Begums, nor did he pretend to try them. With what object, then, did he undertake so long a journey? Evidently in order that he might give, in an irregular

manner, the sanction which in a regular manner he
could not give, to the crimes of those who had recently hired him; and in order that a confused mass
of testimony which he did not sift, which he did not
5 even read, might acquire an authority not properly
belonging to it, from the signature of the highest
judicial functionary in India.

The time was approaching, however, when he was
to be stripped of that robe which has never, since the
10 Revolution, been disgraced so foully as by him. The
state of India had for some time occupied much of
the attention of the British Parliament. Towards the
close of the American war, two committees of the
Commons sat on Eastern affairs. In one Edmund
15 Burke took the lead. The other was under the presidency of the able and versatile Henry Dundas, then
Lord Advocate of Scotland. Great as are the changes
which, during the last sixty years, have taken place in
our Asiatic dominions, the reports which those com-
20 mittees laid on the table of the House will still be
found most interesting and instructive.

There was as yet °no connection between the Company and either of the great parties in the state. The
ministers had no motive to defend Indian abuses.
25 On the contrary, it was for their interest to show, if

possible, that the government and patronage of our Oriental empire might, with advantage, be transferred to themselves. The votes, therefore, which, in consequence of the reports made by the two committees, were passed by the Commons, breathed the spirit of stern and indignant justice. The severest epithets were applied to several of the measures of Hastings, especially to the Rohilla war; and it was resolved, on the motion of Mr. Dundas, that the Company ought to recall a Governor-General who had brought such calamities on the Indian people, and such dishonor on the British name. An act was passed for limiting the jurisdiction of the Supreme Court. The bargain which Hastings had made with the Chief Justice was condemned in the strongest terms; and an address was presented to the king, praying that Impey might be summoned home to answer for his misdeeds.

Impey was recalled by a letter from the Secretary of State. But the proprietors of India Stock resolutely refused to dismiss Hastings from their service, and passed a resolution affirming, what was undeniably true, that they were intrusted by law with the right of naming and removing their Governor-General, and that they were not bound to obey the directions of a single branch of the legislature with respect to such nomination or removal.

Thus supported by his employers, Hastings remained at the head of the government of Bengal till the spring of 1785. His administration, so eventful and stormy, closed in almost perfect quiet. In the Council there was no regular opposition to his measures. Peace was restored to India. The Mahratta war had ceased. Hyder was no more. A treaty had been concluded with his son, Tippoo; and the Carnatic had been evacuated by the armies of Mysore. Since the termination of the American war, England had no European enemy or rival in the Eastern seas.

On a general review of the long administration of Hastings, it is impossible to deny that, against the great crimes by which it is blemished, we have to set off great public services. England had passed through a perilous crisis. She still, indeed, maintained her place in the foremost rank of European powers; and the manner in which she had defended herself against fearful odds had inspired surrounding nations with a high opinion both of her spirit and of her strength. Nevertheless, in every part of the world, except one, she had been a loser. Not only had she been compelled to acknowledge the indepen-

dence of thirteen colonies peopled by her children, and
to conciliate the Irish by giving up the right of legis-
lating for them; but, in the Mediterranean, in the
Gulf of Mexico, on the coast of Africa, on the continent of America, she had been compelled to cede the
fruits of her victories in former wars. Spain regained
Minorca and Florida; France regained Senegal, Goree,
and several West Indian Islands. The only quarter
of the world in which Britain had lost nothing was
the quarter in which her interests had been committed
to the care of Hastings. In spite of the utmost exertions both of European and Asiatic enemies, the power
of our country in the East had been greatly aug-
mented. Benares was subjected; the Nabob Vizier
reduced to vassalage. That our influence had been
thus extended, nay, that Fort William and Fort St.
George had not been occupied by hostile armies, was
owing, if we may trust the general voice of the English in India, to the skill and resolution of Hastings.

His internal administration, with all its blemishes,
gives him a title to be considered as one of the most
remarkable men in our history. He dissolved the
double government. He transferred the direction of
affairs to English hands. Out of a frightful anarchy,
he educed at least a rude and imperfect order. The

K

whole organization by which justice was dispensed, revenue collected, peace maintained throughout a territory not inferior in population to the dominions of Lewis the Sixteenth or of the Emperor Joseph, was formed and superintended by him. He boasted that every public office, without exception, which existed when he left Bengal, was his creation. It is quite true that this system, after all the improvements suggested by the experience of sixty years, still needs improvement, and that it was at first far more defective than it now is. But whoever seriously considers what it is to construct from the beginning the whole of a machine so vast and complex as a government, will allow that what Hastings effected deserves high admiration. To compare the most celebrated European ministers to him seems to us as unjust as it would be to compare the best baker in London with Robinson Crusoe, who, before he could bake a single loaf, had to make his plough and his harrow, his fences and his scarecrows, his sickle and his flail, his mill and his oven.

The just fame of Hastings rises still higher, when we reflect that he was not bred a statesman; that he was sent from school to a counting-house; and that he was employed during the prime of his manhood as a commercial agent, far from all intellectual society.

Nor must we forget that all, or almost all, to whom, when placed at the head of affairs, he could apply for assistance, were persons who owed as little as himself, or less than himself, to education. A minister in Europe finds himself, on the first day on which he commences his functions, surrounded by experienced public servants, the depositaries of official traditions. Hastings had no such help. His own reflection, his own energy, were to supply the place of all Downing Street and Somerset House. Having had no facilities for learning, he was forced to teach. He had first to form himself, and then to form his instruments; and this not in a single department, but in all the departments of the administration.

It must be added that, while engaged in this most arduous task, he was constantly trammelled by orders from home, and frequently borne down by a majority in council. The preservation of an Empire from a formidable combination of foreign enemies, the construction of a government in all its parts, were accomplished by him, while every ship brought out bales of censure from his employers, and while the records of every consultation were filled with acrimonious minutes by his colleagues. We believe that there never was a public man whose temper was so severely tried; not Marlborough, when thwarted by the Dutch Deputies; not Wellington, when he had to deal at once with the Portuguese Regency, the Spanish Juntas, and Mr. Percival. But the temper of Hastings was equal to almost any trial. It was not sweet; but it was calm. Quick and vigorous as his intellect was, the patience with which he endured the most cruel vexations, till a remedy could be found, resembled the patience of stupidity. He seems to have been capable of resentment, bitter and long-enduring; yet his resentment so seldom hurried him into any blunder, that it may be doubted whether what appeared to be revenge was any thing but policy.

The effect of this singular equanimity was that he always had the full command of all the resources of one of the most fertile minds that ever existed. Accordingly no complication of perils and embarrassments could perplex him. For every difficulty he had a contrivance ready; and, whatever may be thought of the justice and humanity of some of his contrivances, it is certain that they seldom failed to serve the purpose for which they were designed.

Together with this extraordinary talent for devising

expedients, Hastings possessed, in a very high degree, another talent scarcely less necessary to a man in his situation; we mean the talent for conducting political controversy. It is as necessary to an English states- man in the East that he should be able to write, as it is to a minister in this country that he should be able to speak. It is chiefly by the oratory of a public man here that the nation judges of his powers. It is from the letters and reports of a public man in India that the dispensers of patronage form their estimate of him. In each case, the talent which receives peculiar encouragement is developed, perhaps at the expense of the other powers. In this country, we sometimes hear men speak above their abilities. It is not very unusual to find gentlemen in the Indian service who write above their abilities. The English politician is a little too much of a debater; the Indian politician a little too much of an essayist.

Of the numerous servants of the Company who have distinguished themselves as framers of minutes and despatches, Hastings stands at the head. He was indeed the person who gave to the official writing of the Indian governments the character which it still retains. He was matched against no common antago- nist. But even Francis was forced to acknowledge,

with sullen and resentful candor, that there was no
contending against the pen of Hastings. And, in
truth, the Governor-General's power of making out a
case, of perplexing what it was inconvenient that
5 people should understand, and of setting in the clearest point of view whatever would bear the light, was
incomparable. His style must be praised with some
reservation. It was in general forcible, pure, and polished; but it was sometimes, though not often, turgid
10 and, on one or two occasions, even bombastic. Perhaps the fondness of Hastings for Persian literature
may have tended to corrupt his taste.

And, since we have referred to his literary tastes,
it would be most unjust not to praise the judicious
15 encouragement which, as a ruler, he gave to liberal
studies and curious researches. His patronage was
extended, with prudent generosity, to voyages, travels,
experiments, publications. He did little, it is true,
towards introducing into India the learning of the
20 West. To make the young natives of Bengal familiar
with Milton and Adam Smith, to substitute the ge-
ography, astronomy, and surgery of Europe for the
dotages of the Brahminical superstition, or for the
imperfect science of ancient Greece transfused through
25 Arabian expositions, this was a scheme reserved to

crown the °beneficent administration of a far more
virtuous ruler. Still it is impossible to refuse high
commendation to a man who, taken from a ledger to
govern an empire, overwhelmed by public business,
surrounded by people as busy as himself, and sepa- 5
rated by thousands of leagues from almost all literary
society, gave, both by his example and by his munificence, a great impulse to learning. In Persian and
Arabic literature he was deeply skilled. With the
Sanscrit he was not himself acquainted; but those 10
who first brought that language to the knowledge of
European students owed much to his encouragement.
It was under his protection that the Asiatic Society
commenced its honorable career. That distinguished
body selected him to be its first president; but, with 15
excellent taste and feeling, he declined the honor in
favor of Sir William Jones. But the chief advantage
which the students of Oriental letters derived from
his patronage remains to be mentioned. The °Pundits
of Bengal had always looked with great jealousy on 20
the attempts of foreigners to pry into those mysteries
which were locked up in the sacred dialect. The
Brahminical religion had been persecuted by the Mahommedans. What the Hindoos knew of the spirit of
the Portuguese government might warrant them in 25

apprehending persecution from Christians. That apprehension the wisdom and moderation of Hastings removed. He was the first foreign ruler who succeeded in gaining the confidence of the hereditary priests of India, and who induced them to lay open to English scholars the secrets of the old Brahminical theology and jurisprudence.

It is indeed impossible to deny that, in the great art of inspiring large masses of human beings with confidence and attachment, no ruler ever surpassed Hastings. If he had made himself popular with the English by giving up the Bengalees to extortion and oppression, or if, on the other hand, he had conciliated the Bengalees and alienated the English, there would have been no cause for wonder. What is peculiar to him is that, being the chief of a small band of strangers who exercised boundless power over a great indigenous population, he made himself beloved both by the subject many and by the dominant few. The affection felt for him by the civil service was singularly ardent and constant. Through all his disasters and perils, his brethren stood by him with steadfast loyalty. The army, at the same time, loved him as armies have seldom loved any but the greatest chiefs who have led them to victory. Even in his disputes with distinguished military men, he could always count on the support of the military profession. While such was his empire over the hearts of his countrymen, he enjoyed among the natives a popularity, such as other governors have perhaps better merited, but such as no other governor has been able to attain. He spoke their vernacular dialects with facility and precision. He was intimately acquainted with their feelings and usages. On one or two occasions, for great ends, he deliberately acted in defiance of their opinion; but on such occasions he gained more in their respect than he lost in their love. In general, he carefully avoided all that could shock their national or religious prejudices. His administration was indeed in many respects faulty; but the Bengalee standard of good government was not high. Under the Nabobs, the hurricane of Mahratta cavalry had passed annually over the rich alluvial plain. But even the Mahratta shrank from a conflict with the mighty children of the sea; and the immense rice harvests of the Lower Ganges were safely gathered in, under the protection of the English sword. The first English conquerors had been more rapacious and merciless even than the Mahrattas; but that generation had passed away. Defective as was the police, heavy as were the public burdens, it is probable that the oldest man in Bengal could not recollect a season of equal security and prosperity. For the first time within living memory, the province was placed under a government strong enough to prevent others from robbing, and not inclined to play the robber itself. These things inspired goodwill. At the same time, the constant success of Hastings and the manner in which he extricated himself from every difficulty made him an object of superstitious admiration; and the more than regal splendor which he sometimes displayed dazzled a people who have much in common with children. Even now, after the lapse of more than fifty years, the natives of India still talk of him as the greatest of the English; and nurses sing children to sleep with a jingling ballad about the fleet horses and richly caparisoned elephants of Sahib Warren Hostein.

The gravest offences of which Hastings was guilty did not affect his popularity with the people of Bengal; for those offences were committed against neighboring states. Those offences, as our readers must have perceived, we are not disposed to vindicate; yet, in order that the censure may be justly apportioned to the transgression, it is fit that the motive of the criminal should be taken into consideration. The motive which prompted the worst acts of Hastings was misdirected and ill-regulated public spirit. The rules of justice, the sentiments of humanity, the plighted faith of treaties, were in his view as nothing, when opposed to the immediate interest of the state. This is no justification, according to the principles either of morality, or of what we believe to be identical with morality, namely, far-sighted policy. Nevertheless the common-sense of mankind, which in questions of this kind seldom goes far wrong, will always recognize a distinction between crimes which originate in an inordinate zeal for the commonwealth, and crimes which originate in selfish cupidity. To the benefit of this distinction Hastings is fairly entitled. There is, we conceive, no reason to suspect that the Rohilla war, the revolution of Benares, or the spoliation of the Princesses of Oude, added a rupee to his fortune. We will not affirm that, in all pecuniary dealings, he showed that punctilious integrity, that dread of the faintest appearance of evil, which is now the glory of the Indian civil service. But when the school in which he had been trained and the temptations to which he was exposed are considered, we are more inclined to praise him for his general uprightness with respect to money, than rigidly to blame him for a

few transactions which would now be called indelicate
and irregular, but which even now would hardly be
designated as corrupt.   A rapacious man he certainly
was not.   Had he been so, he would infallibly have
returned to his country the richest subject in Europe.
We speak within compass, when we say that, without
applying any extraordinary pressure he might easily
have obtained from the °zemindars of the Company's
provinces and from neighboring princes, in the course
of thirteen years, more than three millions sterling,
and might have outshone the splendor of °Carlton
House and of the *Palais Royal*.   He brought home a
fortune such as a Governor-General, fond of state,
and careless of thrift, might easily, during so long a
tenure of office, save out of his legal salary.   Mrs.
Hastings, we are afraid, was less scrupulous.   It was
generally believed that she accepted presents with
great alacrity, and that she thus formed, without the
connivance of her husband, a private hoard amounting
to several lacs of rupees.   We are the more inclined
to give credit to this story, because Mr. Gleig, who
cannot but have heard it, does not, as far as we have
observed, notice or contradict it.

The influence of Mrs. Hastings over her husband
was indeed such that she might easily have obtained

much larger sums than she was ever accused of receiving. At length her health began to give way; and the Governor-General, much against his will, was compelled to send her to England. He seems to have loved her with that love which is peculiar to men of strong minds, to men whose affection is not easily won or widely diffused. The talk of Calcutta ran for some time on the luxurious manner in which he fitted up the round-house of an Indiaman for her accommodation, on the profusion of sandal-wood and carved ivory which adorned her cabin, and on the thousands of rupees which had been expended in order to procure for her the society of an agreeable female companion during the voyage. We may remark here that the letters of Hastings to his wife are exceedingly characteristic. They are tender, and full of indications of esteem and confidence; but, at the same time, a little more ceremonious than is usual in so intimate a relation. The solemn courtesy with which he compliments "his elegant Marian" reminds us now and then of the dignified air with which °Sir Charles Grandison bowed over Miss Byron's hand in the cedar parlor.

After some months, Hastings prepared to follow his wife to England. When it was announced that he was about to quit his office, the feeling of the society

which he had so long governed manifested itself by
many signs. Addresses poured in from Europeans
and Asiatics, from civil functionaries, soldiers, and
traders. On the day on which he delivered up the
5 keys of office, a crowd of friends and admirers formed
a lane to the quay where he embarked. Several
barges escorted him far down the river; and some
attached friends refused to quit him till the low coast
of Bengal was fading from the view, and till the pilot
10 was leaving the ship.

Of his voyage little is known, except that he
amused himself with his books and with his pen; and
that, among the compositions by which he beguiled
the tediousness of that long leisure, was a pleasing
15 imitation of Horace's *Otium Divos rogat*. This little
poem was inscribed to Mr. Shore, afterwards Lord
Teignmouth, a man of whose integrity, humanity, and
honor it is impossible to speak too highly, but who,
like some other excellent members of the civil service,
20 extended to the conduct of his friend Hastings an
indulgence of which his own conduct never stood in
need.

The voyage was, for those times, very speedy. Hastings was little more than four months on the sea. In
25 June, 1785, he landed at Plymouth, posted to London,

appeared at Court, paid his respects in Leadenhall Street, and then retired with his wife to Cheltenham.

He was greatly pleased with his reception. The King treated him with marked distinction. The Queen, who had already incurred much censure on account of the favor which, in spite of the ordinary severity of her virtue, she had shown to the "elegant Marian," was not less gracious to Hastings. The Directors received him in a solemn sitting; and their chairman read to him a vote of thanks which they had passed without one dissentient voice. "I find myself," said Hastings, in a letter written about a quarter of a year after his arrival in England, "I find myself everywhere, and universally, treated with evidences, apparent even to my own observation, that I possess the good opinion of my country."

The confident and exulting tone of his correspondence about this time is the more remarkable, because he had already received ample notice of the attack which was in preparation. Within a week after he landed at Plymouth, Burke gave notice in the House of Commons of a motion seriously affecting a gentleman lately returned from India. The session, however, was then so far advanced, that it was impossible to enter on so extensive and important a subject.

Hastings, it is clear, was not sensible of the danger of his position. Indeed that sagacity, that judgment, that readiness in devising expedients, which had distinguished him in the East, seemed now to have forsaken him; not that his abilities were at all impaired; not that he was not still the same man who had triumphed over Francis and Nuncomar, who had made the Chief Justice and the Nabob Vizier his tools, who had deposed Cheyte Sing, and repelled Hyder Ali. But an oak, as Mr. Grattan finely said, should not be transplanted at fifty. A man who, having left England when a boy, returns to it after thirty or forty years passed in India, will find, be his talents what they may, that he has much both to learn and to unlearn before he can take a place among English statesmen. The working of a representative system, the war of parties, the arts of debate, the influence of the press, are startling novelties to him. Surrounded on every side by new machines and new tactics, he is as much bewildered as Hannibal would have been at Waterloo, or Themistocles at Trafalgar. His very acuteness deludes him. His very vigor causes him to stumble. The more correct his maxims, when applied to the state of society to which he is accustomed, the more certain they are to lead him astray. This was strikingly the case with Hastings. In India he had a bad hand; but he was master of the game, and he won every stake. In England he held excellent cards, if he had known how to play them; and it was chiefly by his own errors that he was brought to the verge of ruin.

Of all his errors the most serious was perhaps the choice of a champion. Clive, in similar circumstances, had made a singularly happy selection. He put himself into the hands of Wedderburn, afterwards Lord Loughborough, one of the few great advocates who have also been great in the House of Commons. To the defence of Clive, therefore, nothing was wanting, neither learning nor knowledge of the world, neither forensic acuteness nor that eloquence which charms political assemblies. Hastings intrusted his interests to a very different person, a major in the Bengal army, named Scott. This gentleman had been sent over from India some time before as an agent of the Governor-General. It was rumored that his services were rewarded with Oriental munificence; and we believe that he received much more than Hastings could conveniently spare. The Major obtained a seat in Parliament, and was there regarded as the organ of his employer. It was evidently impossible that a gentle-

L

man so situated could speak with the authority which belongs to an independent position. Nor had the agent of Hastings the talents necessary for obtaining the ear of an assembly which, accustomed to listen to great orators, had naturally become fastidious. He was always on his legs; he was very tedious; and he had only one topic, the merits and wrongs of Hastings. Everybody who knows the House of Commons will easily guess what followed. The Major was soon considered as the greatest bore of his time. His exertions were not confined to Parliament. There was hardly a day on which the newspapers did not contain some puff upon Hastings, signed *Asiaticus* or *Bengalensis*, but known to be written by the indefatigable Scott; and hardly a month in which some bulky pamphlet on the same subject, and from the same pen, did not pass to the trunkmakers and the pastrycooks. As to this gentleman's capacity for conducting a delicate question through Parliament, our readers will want no evidence beyond that which they will find in letters preserved in these volumes. We will give a single specimen of his temper and judgment. He designated the greatest man then living as "that reptile Mr. Burke."

In spite, however, of this unfortunate choice, the

general aspect of affairs was favorable to Hastings.
The King was on his side. The Company and its
servants were zealous in his cause. Among public
men he had many ardent friends. Such were Lord
Mansfield, who had outlived the vigor of his body, 5
but not that of his mind; and Lord Lansdown, who,
though unconnected with any party, retained the
importance which belongs to great talents and knowledge. The ministers were generally believed to be
favorable to the late Governor-General. They owed 10
their power to the clamor which had been raised
against Mr. Fox's East India Bill. The authors of
that bill, when accused of invading vested rights, and
of setting up powers unknown to the constitution, had
defended themselves by pointing to the crimes of 15
Hastings, and by arguing that abuses so extraordinary
justified extraordinary measures. Those who, by
opposing that bill, had raised themselves to the head
of affairs, would naturally be inclined to extenuate
the evils which had been made the plea for adminis- 20
tering so violent a remedy; and such, in fact, was
their general disposition. The Lord Chancellor Thurlow, in particular, whose great place and force of
intellect gave him a weight in the government inferior only to that of Mr. Pitt, espoused the cause of 25

Hastings with indecorous violence. Mr. Pitt, though
he had censured many parts of the Indian system,
had studiously abstained from saying a word against
the late chief of the Indian government. To Major
5 Scott, indeed, the °young minister had in private
extolled Hastings as a great, a wonderful man, who
had the highest claims on the government. There
was only one objection to granting all that so eminent
a servant of the public could ask. The resolution of
10 censure still remained on the journals of the House of
Commons. That resolution was, indeed, unjust; but,
till it was rescinded, could the minister advise the
King to bestow any mark of approbation on the person
censured? If Major Scott is to be trusted, Mr. Pitt
15 declared that this was the only reason which prevented the advisers of the Crown from conferring a
peerage on the late Governor-General. Mr. Dundas
was the only important member of the administration
who was deeply committed to a different view of the
20 subject. He had moved the resolution which created
the difficulty; but even from him little was to be
apprehended. Since he had presided over the committee on Eastern affairs, the great changes had taken
place. He was surrounded by new allies; he had
25 fixed his hopes on new objects; and whatever may

have been his good qualities, — and he had many, — flattery itself never reckoned rigid consistency in the number.

From the ministry, therefore, Hastings had every reason to expect support; and the ministry was very powerful. The opposition was loud and vehement against him. But the opposition, though formidable from the wealth and influence of some of its members, and from the admirable talents and eloquence of others, was outnumbered in Parliament, and odious throughout the country. Nor, as far as we can judge, was the opposition generally desirous to engage in so serious an undertaking as the impeachment of an Indian Governor. Such an impeachment must last for years. It must impose on the chiefs of the party an immense load of labor. Yet it could scarcely, in any manner, affect the event of the great political game. The followers of the coalition were therefore more inclined to revile Hastings than to prosecute him. They lost no opportunity of coupling his name with the names of the most hateful tyrants of whom history makes mention. The wits of °Brooks's aimed their keenest sarcasms both at his public and at his domestic life. Some fine diamonds which he had presented, as it was rumored, to the royal family,

and a certain richly carved ivory bed which the Queen
had done him the honor to accept from him, were
favorite subjects of ridicule.   One lively poet proposed that the great acts of the fair Marian's pres-
5 ent husband should be immortalized by the pencil of
his predecessor; and that Imhoff should be employed
to embellish the House of Commons with paintings
of the bleeding Rohillas, of Nuncomar swinging, of
Cheyte Sing letting himself down to the Ganges.
10 Another, in an exquisitely humorous parody of Virgil's
third eclogue, propounded the question, what that min-
eral could be of which the rays had power to make
the most austere of princesses the friend of a wanton.
A third described, with gay malevolence, the gorgeous
15 appearance of Mrs. Hastings at St. James's, the galaxy
of jewels, torn from Indian Begums, which adorned
her head dress, her necklace gleaming with future
votes, and the depending questions that shone upon
her ears.   Satirical attacks of this description, and
20 perhaps a motion for a vote of censure, would have
satisfied the great body of the opposition.   But there
were two men whose indignation was not to be so
appeased, Philip Francis and °Edmund Burke.

Francis had recently entered the House of Com-
25 mons, and had already established a character there

for industry and ability. He labored indeed under one most unfortunate defect, want of fluency. But he occasionally expressed himself with a dignity and energy worthy of the greatest orators. Before he had been many days in Parliament, he incurred the bitter dislike of Pitt, who constantly treated him with as much asperity as the laws of debate would allow. Neither lapse of years nor change of scene had mitigated the enmities which Francis had brought back from the East. After his usual fashion, he mistook his malevolence for virtue, nursed it, as preachers tell us that we ought to nurse our good dispositions, and paraded it on all occasions with Pharisaical ostentation.

The zeal of Burke was still fiercer; but it was far purer. Men unable to understand the elevation of his mind have tried to find out some discreditable motive for the vehemence and pertinacity which he showed on this occasion. But they have altogether failed. The idle story that he had some private slight to revenge has long been given up, even by the advocates of Hastings. Mr. Gleig supposes that Burke was actuated by party spirit, that he retained a bitter remembrance of the fall of the coalition, that he attributed that fall to the exertions of the East India interest, and that he considered Hastings as the head and the representative

of that interest. This explanation seems to be sufficiently refuted by a reference to dates. The hostility
of Burke to Hastings commenced long before the coalition; and lasted long after Burke had become a stren-
5 uous supporter of those by whom the coalition had
been defeated. It began when Burke and Fox, closely
allied together, were attacking the influence of the
crown, and calling for peace with the American republic. It continued till Burke, alienated from Fox, and
10 loaded with the favors of the crown, died, preaching a
crusade against the French republic. We surely cannot attribute to the events of 1784 an enmity which
began in 1781, and which retained undiminished force
long after persons far more deeply implicated than
15 Hastings in the events of 1784 had been cordially for-
given. And why should we look for any other explanation of Burke's conduct than that which we find on
the surface? The plain truth is that Hastings had
committed some great crimes, and that the thought of
20 those crimes made the blood of Burke boil in his veins.
For Burke was a man in whom compassion for suffering, and hatred of injustice and tyranny, were as
strong as in °Las Casas or Clarkson. And although in
him, as in Las Casas and in Clarkson, these noble feel-
25 ings were alloyed with the infirmity which belongs to

human nature, he is, like them, entitled to this great
praise, that he devoted years of intense labor to the
service of a people with whom he had neither blood
nor language, neither religion nor manners in common,
and from whom no requital, no thanks, no applause 5
could be expected.

His knowledge of India was such as few, even of
those Europeans who have passed many years in that
country, have attained, and such as certainly was
never attained by any public man who had not quitted 10
Europe. He had studied the history, the laws, and
the usages of the East with an industry, such as is
seldom found united to so much genius and so much
sensibility. Others have perhaps been equally labori-
ous, and have collected an equal mass of materials. 15
But the manner in which Burke brought his higher
powers of intellect to work on statements of facts,
and on tables of figures, was peculiar to himself. In
every part of those huge bales of Indian information
which repelled almost all other readers, his mind, at 20
once philosophical and poetical, found something to
instruct or to delight. His reason analyzed and
digested those vast and shapeless masses; his imagination animated and colored them. Out of darkness,
and dulness, and confusion, he formed a multitude 25

of ingenious theories and vivid pictures. He had, in
the highest degree, that noble faculty whereby man
is able to live in the past and in the future, in the
distant and in the unreal. India and its inhabitants
5 were not to him, as to most Englishmen, mere names
and abstractions, but a real country and a real people.
The burning sun, the strange vegetation of the palm
and the cocoa tree, the rice-field, the tank, the huge
trees, older than the Mogul empire, under which the
10 village crowds assemble, the thatched roof of the
peasant's hut, the rich tracery of the mosque where
the imaum prays with his face to Mecca, the drums,
and banners, and gaudy idols, the devotee swinging
in the air, the graceful maiden, with the pitcher on
15 her head, descending the steps to the river-side, the
black faces, the long beards, the yellow streaks of
sect, the turbans and the flowing robes, the spears
and the silver maces, the elephants with their can-
opies of state, the gorgeous palanquin of the prince,
20 and the close litter of the noble lady, all these things
were to him as the objects amidst which his own life
had been passed, as the objects which lay on the road
between Beaconsfield and St. James's Street. All
India was present to the eye of his mind, from the
25 halls where suitors laid gold and perfumes at the feet

of sovereigns to the wild moor where the gypsy camp
was pitched, from the bazaar, humming like a bee-hive
with the crowd of buyers and sellers, to the jungle
where the lonely courier shakes his bunch of iron
rings to scare away the hyænas. He had just as
lively an idea of the insurrection at Benares as of
Lord George Gordon's riots, and of the execution of
Nuncomar as of the execution of Dr. Dodd. Oppression in Bengal was to him the same thing as oppression in the °streets of London.

He saw that Hastings had been guilty of some most
unjustifiable acts. All that followed was natural and
necessary in a mind like Burke's. His imagination
and his passions, once excited, hurried him beyond
the bounds of justice and good sense. His reason,
powerful as it was, became the slave of feelings which
it should have controlled. His indignation, virtuous
in its origin, acquired too much of the character of
personal aversion. He could see no mitigating circumstance, no redeeming merit. His temper, which,
though generous and affectionate, had always been
irritable, had now been made almost savage by bodily
infirmities and mental vexations. Conscious of great
powers and great virtues, he found himself, in age
and poverty, a mark for the hatred of a perfidious

court and a deluded people. In Parliament his eloquence was out of date. A young generation, which
knew him not, had filled the House. Whenever he
rose to speak, his voice was drowned by the unseemly
interruption of lads who were in their cradles when
his orations on the °Stamp Act called forth the ap
plause of the great Earl of Chatham. These things
had produced on his proud and sensitive spirit an
effect at which we cannot wonder. He could no
longer discuss any question with calmness, or make
allowance for honest differences of opinion. Those
who think that he was more violent and acrimonious
in debates about India than on other occasions are ill
informed respecting the last years of his life. In the
discussions on the Commercial Treaty with the Court
of Versailles, on the Regency, on the French Revolution, he showed even more virulence than in conducting the impeachment. Indeed it may be remarked
that the very persons who call him a mischievous
maniac, for condemning in burning words the Rohilla
war and the spoliation of the Begums, exalted him
into a prophet as soon as he began to declaim, with
greater vehemence, and not with greater reason,
against the taking of the Bastile and the insults
offered to Marie Antoinette. To us he appears to

have been neither a maniac in the former case, nor a prophet in the latter, but in both cases a great and good man, led into extravagance by a sensibility which domineered over all his faculties.

It may be doubted whether the personal antipathy of Francis or the nobler indignation of Burke, would have led their party to adopt extreme measures against Hastings, if his own conduct had been judicious. He should have felt that, great as his public services had been, he was not faultless, and should have been content to make his escape, without aspiring to the honors of a triumph. He and his agent took a different view. They were impatient for the rewards which, as they conceived, were deferred only till Burke's attack should be over. They accordingly resolved to force on a decisive action with an enemy for whom, if they had been wise, they would have made a bridge of gold. On the first day of the session in 1786, Major Scott reminded Burke of the notice given in the preceding year, and asked whether it was seriously intended to bring any charge against the late Governor-General. This challenge left no course open to the Opposition, except to come forward as accusers, or to acknowledge themselves calumniators. The administration of Hastings had not been so

blameless, nor was the great party of Fox and North so feeble, that it could be prudent to venture on so bold a defiance. The leaders of the Opposition instantly returned the only answer which they could
5 with honor return; and the whole party was irrevocably pledged to a prosecution.

Burke began his operations by applying for Papers. Some of the documents for which he asked were refused by the ministers, who, in the debate, held
10 language such as strongly confirmed the prevailing opinion, that they intended to support Hastings. In April, the charges were laid on the table. They had been drawn by Burke with great ability, though in a form too much resembling that of a pamphlet.
15 Hastings was furnished with a copy of the accusation; and it was intimated to him that he might, if he thought fit, be heard in his own defence at the bar of the Commons.

Here again Hastings was pursued by the same
20 fatality which had attended him ever since the day when he set foot on English ground. It seemed to be decreed that this man, so politic and so successful in the East, should commit nothing but blunders in Europe. Any judicious adviser would have told
25 him that the best thing which he could do would be

to make an eloquent, forcible, and affecting oration at the bar of the House; but that, if he could not trust himself to speak, and found it necessary to read, he ought to be as concise as possible. Audiences accustomed to extemporaneous debating of the highest excellence are always impatient of long written compositions. Hastings, however, sat down as he would have done at the Government-house in Bengal, and prepared a paper of immense length. That paper, if recorded on the consultations of an Indian administration, would have been justly praised as a very able minute. But it was now out of place. It fell flat, as the best written defence must have fallen flat, on an assembly accustomed to the animated and strenuous conflicts of Pitt and Fox. The members, as soon as their curiosity about the face and demeanor of so eminent a stranger was satisfied, walked away to dinner, and left Hastings to tell his story till midnight to the clerks and the Serjeant-at-arms.

All preliminary steps having been duly taken, Burke, in the beginning of June, brought forward the charge relating to the Rohilla war. He acted discreetly in placing this accusation in the van; for Dundas had formerly moved, and the House had adopted, a resolution condemning, in the most severe terms, the policy followed by Hastings with regard to Rohilcund. Dundas had little, or rather nothing, to say in defence of his own consistency; but he put a bold face on the matter, and opposed the motion. Among other things, he declared that, though he still thought the Rohilla war unjustifiable, he considered the services which Hastings had subsequently rendered to the state as sufficient to atone even for so great an offence. Pitt did not speak, but voted with Dundas; and Hastings was absolved by a hundred and nineteen votes against sixty-seven.

Hastings was now confident of victory. It seemed, indeed, that he had reason to be so. The Rohilla war was, of all his measures, that which his accusers might with greatest advantage assail. It had been condemned by the Court of Directors. It had been condemned by the House of Commons. It had been condemned by Mr. Dundas, who had since become the chief minister of the Crown for Indian affairs. Yet Burke, having chosen this strong ground, had been completely defeated on it. That, having failed here, he should succeed on any point, was generally thought impossible. It was rumored at the clubs and coffee-houses that one or perhaps two more charges would be brought forward; that if, on those charges, the sense of the House of Commons should be against impeachment, the Opposition would let the matter drop, that Hastings would be immediately raised to the peerage, decorated with the star of the Bath, °sworn of the privy council, and invited to lend the ₅ assistance of his talents and experience to the India board. Lord Thurlow, indeed, some months before, had spoken with contempt of the scruples which prevented Pitt from calling Hastings to the House of Lords; and had even said that, if the Chancellor of ₁₀ the Exchequer was afraid of the Commons, there was nothing to prevent the Keeper of the Great Seal from taking the royal pleasure about a patent of peerage. The very title was chosen. Hastings was to be Lord Daylesford. For, through all changes of scene and changes ₁₅ of fortune, remained unchanged his attachment to the spot which had witnessed the greatness and the fall of his family, and which had borne so great a part in the first dreams of his young ambition.

But in a very few days these fair prospects were ₂₀ overcast. On the thirteenth of June, Mr. Fox brought forward, with great ability and eloquence, the charge respecting the treatment of Cheyte Sing. Francis followed on the same side. The friends of Hastings were in high spirits when Pitt rose. With his usual ₂₅

M

abundance and felicity of language, the Minister gave
his opinion on the case. He maintained that the
Governor-General was justified in calling on the
Rajah of Benares for pecuniary assistance, and in
imposing a fine when that assistance was contuma-
ciously withheld. He also thought that the conduct
of the Governor-General during the insurrection had
been distinguished by ability and presence of mind.
He censured, with great bitterness, the conduct of
Francis, both in India and in Parliament, as most
dishonest and malignant. The necessary inference
from Pitt's arguments seemed to be that Hastings
ought to be honorably acquitted; and both the friends
and the opponents of the Minister expected from him
a declaration to that effect. To the astonishment of
all parties, he concluded by saying that, though he
thought it right in Hastings to fine Cheyte Sing for
contumacy, yet the amount of the fine was too great
for the occasion. On this ground, and on this ground
alone, did Mr. Pitt, applauding every other part of the
conduct of Hastings with regard to Benares, declare
that he should vote in favor of Mr. Fox's motion.

The House was thunderstruck; and it well might be
so. For the wrong done to Cheyte Sing, even had it
been as flagitious as Fox and Francis contended, was

a trifle when compared with the horrors which had been inflicted on Rohilcund. But if Mr. Pitt's view of the case of Cheyte Sing were correct, there was no ground for an impeachment, or even for a vote of censure. If the offence of Hastings was really no more than this, that, having a right to impose a mulct, the amount of which mulct was not defined, but was left to be settled by his discretion, he had, not for his own advantage, but for that of the state, demanded too much, was this an offence which required a criminal proceeding of the highest solemnity, a criminal proceeding, to which, during sixty years, no public functionary had been subjected? We can see, we think, in what way a man of sense and integrity might have been induced to take any course respecting Hastings, except the course which Mr. Pitt took. Such a man might have thought a great example necessary, for the preventing of injustice, and for the vindicating of the national honor, and might, on that ground, have voted for impeachment both on the Rohilla charge, and on the Benares charge. Such a man might have thought that the offences of Hastings had been atoned for by great services, and might, on that ground, have voted against the impeachment, on both charges. With great diffidence, we give it as our opinion that the most cor-

rect course would, on the whole, have been to impeach
on the Rohilla charge, and to acquit on the Benares
charge. Had the Benares charge appeared to us in
the same light in which it appeared to Mr. Pitt, we
should without hesitation have voted for acquittal
on that charge. The one course which it is incon-
ceivable that any man of a tenth part of Mr. Pitt's
abilities can have honestly taken was the course
which he took. He acquitted Hastings on the Rohilla
charge. He softened down the Benares charge till
it became no charge at all; and then he pronounced
that it contained matter for impeachment.

Nor must it be forgotten that the principal reason
assigned by the ministry for not impeaching Hastings
on account of the Rohilla war was this, that the delin-
quencies of the early part of his administration had
been atoned for by the excellence of the later part.
Was it not most extraordinary that men who had held
this language could afterwards vote that the later
part of his administration furnished matter for no less
than twenty articles of impeachment? They first
represented the conduct of Hastings in 1780 and 1781
as so highly meritorious that, like works of super-
erogation in the Catholic theology, it ought to be
efficacious for the cancelling of former offences; and

they then prosecuted him for his conduct in 1780 and 1781.

The general astonishment was the greater, because, only twenty-four hours before, the members on whom the minister could depend had received the usual notes from the Treasury, begging them to be in their places and to vote against Mr. Fox's motion. It was asserted by Mr. Hastings, that, early on the morning of the very day on which the debate took place, Dundas called on Pitt, woke him, and was closeted with him many hours. The result of this conference was a determination to give up the late Governor-General to the vengeance of the Opposition. It was impossible even for the most powerful minister to carry all his followers with him in so strange a course. Several persons high in office, the Attorney-General, Mr. Grenville, and Lord Mulgrave, divided against Mr. Pitt. But the devoted adherents who stood by the head of the government without asking questions, were sufficiently numerous to turn the scale. A hundred and nineteen members voted for Mr. Fox's motion; seventy-nine against it. Dundas silently followed Pitt.

That good and great man, the late William Wilberforce, often related the events of this remarkable night. He described the amazement of the House, and the bitter reflections which were muttered against the Prime Minister by some of the habitual supporters of government. Pitt himself appeared to feel that 5 his conduct required some explanation. He left the treasury bench, sat for some time next to Mr. Wilberforce, and very earnestly declared that he had found it impossible, as a man of conscience, to stand any longer by Hastings. The business, he said, was too 10 bad. Mr. Wilberforce, we are bound to add, fully believed that his friend was sincere, and that the suspicions to which this mysterious affair gave rise were altogether unfounded.

Those suspicions, indeed, were such as it is painful 15 to mention. The friends of Hastings, most of whom, it is to be observed, generally supported the administration, affirmed that the motive of Pitt and Dundas was jealousy. Hastings was personally a favorite with the King. He was the idol of the East India 20 Company and of its servants. If he were absolved by the Commons, seated among the Lords, admitted to the Board of Control, closely allied with the strong-minded and imperious Thurlow, was it not almost certain that he would soon draw to himself the entire 25 management of Eastern affairs? Was it not possible that he might become a formidable rival in the cabinet? It had probably got abroad that very singular communications had taken place between Thurlow and Major Scott, and that, if the °First Lord of the Treasury was afraid to recommend Hastings for a peerage, the °Chancellor was ready to take the responsibility of that step on himself. Of all ministers, Pitt was the least likely to submit with patience to such an encroachment on his functions. If the Commons impeached Hastings, all danger was at an end. The proceeding, however it might terminate, would probably last some years. In the meantime, the accused person would be excluded from honors and public employments, and could scarcely venture even to pay his duty at court. Such were the motives attributed by a great part of the public to the young minister, whose ruling passion was generally believed to be avarice of power.

The °prorogation soon interrupted the discussions respecting Hastings. In the following year, those discussions were resumed. The charge touching the spoliation of the Begums was brought forward by Sheridan, in a speech which was so imperfectly reported that it may be said to be wholly lost, but which was, without doubt, the most elaborately brilliant of all the productions of his ingenious mind. The impression which it produced was such as has never been equalled. He sat down, not merely amidst cheering, but amidst the loud clapping of hands, in which the Lords below the bar and the strangers in the gallery joined. The excitement of the House was such that no other speaker could obtain a hearing; and the debate was adjourned. The ferment spread fast through the town. Within four and twenty hours, Sheridan was offered a thousand pounds for the copyright of the speech, if he would himself correct it for the press. The impression made by this remarkable display of eloquence on severe and experienced critics, whose discernment may be supposed to have been quickened by emulation, was deep and permanent. Mr. Windham, twenty years later, said that the speech deserved all its fame, and was, in spite of some faults of taste, such as were seldom wanting either in the literary or in the parliamentary performances of Sheridan, the finest that had been delivered within the memory of man. Mr. Fox, about the same time, being asked by the late Lord Holland what was the best speech ever made in the House of Commons, assigned the first place, without hesitation, to the great oration of Sheridan on the Oude charge.

When the debate was resumed, the tide ran so strongly against the accused that his friends were coughed and scraped down. Pitt declared himself for Sheridan's motion; and the question was carried by a hundred and seventy-five votes against sixty-eight. 5

The Opposition, flushed with victory and strongly supported by the public sympathy, proceeded to bring forward a succession of charges relating chiefly to pecuniary transactions. The friends of Hastings were discouraged, and having now no hope of being 10 able to avert an impeachment, were not very strenuous in their exertions. At length the House, having agreed to twenty articles of charge, directed Burke to go before the Lords, and to impeach the late Governor-General of High Crimes and Misdemeanors. Hastings 15 was at the same time arrested by the Serjeant-at-arms, and carried to the bar of the Peers.

The session was now within ten days of its close. It was, therefore, impossible that any progress could be made in the trial till the next year. Hastings was 20 admitted to bail; and further proceedings were postponed till the Houses should re-assemble.

When Parliament met in the following winter, the Commons proceeded to elect a committee for managing the impeachment. Burke stood at the head; and 25

with him were associated most of the leading members of the Opposition. But when the name of Francis was read a fierce contention arose. It was said
that Francis and Hastings were notoriously on bad
5 terms, that they had been at feud during many years,
that on one occasion their mutual aversion had impelled them to seek each other's lives, and that it
would be improper and indelicate to select a private
enemy to be a public accuser. It was urged on the
10 other side with great force, particularly by Mr. Windham, that impartiality, though the first duty of a
judge, had never been reckoned among the qualities
of an advocate; that in the ordinary administration
of criminal justice among the English, the aggrieved
15 party, the very last person who ought to be admitted
into the jury-box, is the prosecutor; that what was
wanted in a manager was, not that he should be free
from bias, but that he should be able, well informed,
energetic, and active. The ability and information
20 of Francis were admitted; and the very animosity
with which he was reproached, whether a virtue or a
vice, was at least a pledge for his energy and activity.
It seems difficult to refute these arguments. But the
inveterate hatred borne by Francis to Hastings had
25 excited general disgust. The House decided that

Francis should not be a manager. Pitt voted with the majority, Dundas with the minority.

In the mean time, the preparations for the trial had proceeded rapidly; and on the 13th of February, 1788, the sittings of the Court commenced. There have been spectacles more dazzling to the eye, more gorgeous with jewelry and cloth of gold, more attractive to grown-up children, than that which was then exhibited at Westminster; but, perhaps, there never was a spectacle so well calculated to strike a highly cultivated, a reflecting, and imaginative mind. All the various kinds of interest which belong to the near and to the distant, to the present and to the past, were collected on one spot, and in one hour. All the talents and all the accomplishments which are developed by liberty and civilization were now displayed, with every advantage that could be derived both from co-operation and from contrast. Every step in the proceedings carried the mind either backward, through many troubled centuries, to the days when the foundations of our constitution were laid; or far away, over boundless seas and deserts, to dusky nations living under strange stars, worshipping strange gods, and writing strange characters from right to left. The °High Court of Parliament was to sit, according

to forms handed down from the days of the Plantage-
nets, on an Englishman accused of exercising tyranny
over the lord of the holy city of Benares, and over the
ladies of the princely house of Oude.

5   The place was worthy of such a trial. It was the
great °hall of William Rufus, the hall which had
resounded with acclamations at the inauguration of
thirty kings, the hall which had witnessed the just
sentence of Bacon and the just absolution of Somers,
10 the hall where the eloquence of Strafford had for a
moment awed and melted a victorious party inflamed
with just resentment, the hall where Charles had confronted the High Court of Justice with the placid
courage which has half redeemed his fame. Neither
15 military nor civil pomp was wanting. The avenues
were lined with grenadiers. The streets were kept
clear by cavalry. The peers, robed in gold and
ermine, were marshalled by the heralds under °Gar-
ter King-at-arms. The judges in their vestments
20 of state attended to give advice on points of law.
Near a hundred and seventy lords, three fourths of
the Upper House as the Upper House then was,
walked in solemn order from their usual place of
assembling to the tribunal. The junior Baron pres-
25 ent led the way, George Eliott, Lord Heathfield,

recently ennobled for his memorable defence of Gibraltar against the fleets and armies of France and Spain. The long procession was closed by the Duke of Norfolk, Earl Marshal of the realm, by the great dignitaries, and by the brothers and sons of the King. Last of all came the Prince of Wales, conspicuous by his fine person and noble bearing. The gray old walls were hung with scarlet. The long galleries were crowded by an audience such as has rarely excited the fears or the emulation of an orator. There were gathered together, from all parts of a great, free, enlightened, and prosperous empire, grace and female loveliness, wit and learning, the representatives of every science and of every art. There were seated round the Queen the fair-haired young daughters of the house of Brunswick. There the Ambassadors of great Kings and Commonwealths gazed with admiration on a spectacle which no other country in the world could present. There °Siddons, in the prime of her majestic beauty, looked with emotion on a scene surpassing all the imitations of the stage. There the °historian of the Roman Empire thought of the days when Cicero pleaded the cause of Sicily against Verres, and when, before a senate which still retained some show of freedom, Tacitus thundered against the

oppressor of Africa.   There were seen, side by side,
the °greatest painter and the °greatest scholar of the
age.   The spectacle had allured Reynolds from that
easel which has preserved to us the thoughtful fore-
heads of so many writers and statesmen, and the
sweet smiles of so many noble matrons.   It had
induced Parr to suspend his labors in that dark and
profound mine from which he had extracted a vast
treasure of erudition, a treasure too often buried in
10 the earth, too often paraded with injudicious and
inelegant ostentation, but still precious, massive, and
splendid.   There appeared the voluptuous charms of
her to whom the heir of the throne had in secret
°plighted his faith.   There too was she, the beautiful
15 mother of a beautiful race, the °Saint Cecilia whose
delicate features, lighted up by love and music, art
has rescued from the common decay.   There were
the members of that brilliant society which quoted,
criticised, and exchanged repartees, under the rich
20 peacock-hangings of °Mrs. Montague.   And there the
ladies whose lips, more persuasive than those of Fox
himself, had carried the Westminster election against
palace and treasury, shone round °Georgiana Duchess
of Devonshire.

25   The Serjeants made proclamation.   Hastings ad-

vanced to the bar, and bent his knee. The culprit was indeed not unworthy of that great presence. He had ruled an extensive and populous country, had made laws and treaties, had sent forth armies, had set up and pulled down princes. And in his high place he had so borne himself, that all had feared him, that most had loved him, and that hatred itself could deny him no title to glory, except virtue. He looked like a great man, and not like a bad man. A person small and emaciated, yet deriving dignity from a carriage which, while it indicated deference to the court, indicated also habitual self-possession and self-respect, a high and intellectual forehead, a brow pensive, but not gloomy, a mouth of inflexible decision, a face pale and worn, but serene, on which was written, as legibly as under the picture in the council-chamber at Calcutta, °*Mens aequa in arduis ;* such was the aspect with which the great Proconsul presented himself to his judges.

His counsel accompanied him, men all of whom were afterwards raised by their talents and learning to the highest posts in their profession, the bold and strong-minded Law, afterwards Chief Justice of the King's Bench; the more humane and eloquent Dallas, afterwards Chief Justice of the Common Pleas; and

Plomer who, near twenty years later, successfully con-
ducted in the same high court the defence of Lord
Melville, and subsequently became Vice-chancellor and
Master of the Rolls.

5   But neither the culprit nor his advocates attracted
so much notice as the accusers. In the midst of the
blaze of red drapery, a space has been fitted up with
green benches and tables for the Commons. The
managers, with Burke at their head, appeared in full
10 dress. The collectors of gossip did not fail to remark
that even Fox, generally so regardless of his appearance, had paid to the illustrious tribunal the compliment of wearing a °bag and sword. Pitt had refused
to be one of the conductors of the impeachment; and
15 his commanding, copious, and sonorous eloquence was
wanting to that great muster of various talents. Age
and blindness had unfitted Lord North for the duties
of a public prosecutor; and his friends were left without the help of his excellent sense, his tact, and his
20 urbanity. But, in spite of the absence of these two
distinguished members of the Lower House, the box
in which the managers stood contained an array of
speakers such as perhaps had not appeared together
since the great age of Athenian eloquence. There
25 were °Fox and Sheridan, the English Demosthenes

and the English Hyperides. There was Burke, ignorant, indeed, or negligent of the art of adapting his
reasonings and his style to the capacity and taste of
his hearers, but in amplitude of comprehension and
richness of imagination superior to every orator, 5
ancient or modern. There, with eyes reverentially
fixed on Burke, appeared the finest gentleman of the
age, his form developed by every manly exercise, his
face beaming with intelligence and spirit, the ingenious, the chivalrous, the high-souled Windham. Nor, 10
though surrounded by such men, did the youngest
manager pass unnoticed. At an age when most of
those who distinguish themselves in life are still contending for prizes and fellowships at college, he had
won for himself a conspicuous place in Parliament. 15
No advantage of fortune or connection was wanting
that could set off to the height his splendid talents
and his unblemished honor. At twenty-three he had
been thought worthy to be ranked with the veteran
statesmen who appeared as the delegates of the British 20
Commons, at the bar of the British nobility. All who
stood at that bar, save him alone, are gone, culprit,
advocates, accusers. To the generation which is now
in the vigor of life, he is the sole representative of
a great age which has passed away. But those who, 25

N

within the last ten years, have listened with delight,
till the °morning sun shone on the tapestries of the
House of Lords, to the lofty and animated eloquence
of °Charles Earl Grey, are able to form some estimate
5 of the powers of a race of men among whom he was
not the foremost.

The charges and the answers of Hastings were first
read. The ceremony occupied two whole days, and
was rendered less tedious than it would otherwise
10 have been by the silver voice and just emphasis of
Cowper, the clerk of the court, a near relation of the
amiable poet. On the third day Burke rose. Four
sittings were occupied by his opening speech, which
was intended to be a general introduction to all the
15 charges. With an exuberance of thought and a splendor of diction which more than satisfied the highly
raised expectation of the audience, he described the
character and institutions of the natives of India,
recounted the circumstances in which the Asiatic
20 empire of Britain had originated, and set forth the
constitution of the Company and of the English
Presidencies. Having thus attempted to communi-
cate to his hearers an idea of Eastern society, as
vivid as that which existed in his own mind, he pro-
25 ceeded to arraign the administration of Hastings as

systematically conducted in defiance of morality and
public law. The energy and pathos of the great
orator extorted expressions of unwonted admiration
from the stern and hostile Chancellor, and, for a
moment, seemed to pierce even the resolute heart of
the defendant. The ladies in the galleries, unaccustomed to such displays of eloquence, excited by the
solemnity of the occasion, and perhaps not unwilling
to display their °taste and sensibility, were in a state
of uncontrollable emotion. Handkerchiefs were pulled
out; smelling-bottles were handed round; hysterical
sobs and screams were heard; and Mrs. Sheridan was
carried out in a fit. At length the orator concluded.
Raising his voice till the old arches of Irish oak
resounded, "Therefore," said he, "hath it with all
confidence been ordered by the Commons of Great
Britain, that I impeach Warren Hastings of high
crimes and misdemeanors. I impeach him in the
name of the Commons' House of Parliament, whose
trust he has betrayed. I impeach him in the name
of the English nation, whose ancient honor he has
sullied. I impeach him in the name of the people
of India, whose rights he has trodden under foot, and
whose country he has turned into a desert. Lastly, in
the name of human nature itself, in the name of both

sexes, in the name of every age, in the name of every rank, I impeach the common enemy and oppressor of all!"

When the deep murmur of various emotions had subsided, Mr. Fox rose to address the Lords respecting the course of proceeding to be followed. The wish of the accusers was that the Court would bring to a close the investigation of the first charge before the second was opened. The wish of Hastings and of his counsel was that the managers should open all the charges, and produce all the evidence for the prosecution, before the defence began. The Lords retired to their own House to consider the question. The Chancellor took the side of Hastings. Lord Loughborough, who was now in opposition, supported the demand of the managers. The division showed which way the inclination of the tribunal leaned. A majority of near three to one decided in favor of the course for which Hastings contended.

When the Court sat again, Mr. Fox, assisted by Mr. Grey, opened the charge respecting Cheyte Sing, and several days were spent in reading papers and hearing witnesses. The next article was that relating to the Princesses of Oude. The conduct of this part of the case was intrusted to Sheridan. The curiosity of

the public to hear him was unbounded. His spark-
ling and highly finished declamation lasted two days;
but the Hall was crowded to suffocation during the
whole time. It was said that fifty guineas had been
paid for a single ticket. Sheridan, when he con- 5
cluded, contrived, with a knowledge of stage effect
which his father might have envied, to sink back, as
if exhausted, into the arms of Burke, who hugged
him with the energy of generous admiration.

June was now far advanced. The session could not 10
last much longer; and the progress which had been
made in the impeachment was not very satisfactory.
There were twenty charges. On two only of these
had even the case for the prosecution been heard; and
it was now a year since Hastings had been admitted 15
to bail.

The interest taken by the public in the trial was
great when the Court began to sit, and rose to the
height when Sheridan spoke on the charge relating to
the Begums. From that time the excitement went 20
down fast. The spectacle had lost the attraction of
novelty. The great displays of rhetoric were over.
What was behind was not of a nature to entice men
of letters from their books in the morning, or to tempt
ladies who had left the masquerade at two to be out 25

of bed before eight. There remained examinations
and cross-examinations. There remained statements
of accounts. There remained the reading of papers,
filled with words unintelligible to English ears, with
lacs and crores, zemindars and aumils, sunnuds and
perwannahs, jaghires and nuzzurs. There remained
bickerings, not always carried on with the best taste
or with the best temper, between the managers of the
impeachment and the counsel for the defence, particularly between Mr. Burke and Mr. Law. There remained the endless marches and countermarches of
the Peers between their House and the Hall; for as
often as a point of law was to be discussed, their Lordships retired to discuss it apart; and the consequence
was, as a Peer wittily said, that the judges walked and
the trial stood still.

It is to be added that, in the spring of 1788, when
the trial commenced, no important question, either of
domestic or foreign policy, occupied the public mind.
The proceeding in Westminster Hall, therefore, naturally attracted most of the attention of Parliament
and of the country. It was the one great event of
that season. But in the following year the King's
illness, the debates on the Regency, the expectation
of a change of ministry, completely diverted public

attention from Indian affairs; and within a fortnight after George the Third had returned thanks in St Paul's for his recovery, the States-General of France met at Versailles. In the midst of the agitation produced by these events, the impeachment was for a time almost forgotten.

The trial in the Hall went on languidly. In the session of 1788, when the proceedings had the interest of novelty, and when the Peers had little other business before them, only thirty-five days were given to the impeachment. In 1789, the Regency Bill occupied the Upper House till the session was far advanced. When the King recovered the circuits were beginning. The judges left town; the Lords waited for the return of the oracles of jurisprudence; and the consequence was that during the whole year only seventeen days were given to the case of Hastings. It was clear that the matter would be protracted to a length unprecedented in the annals of criminal law.

In truth, it is impossible to deny that impeachment, though it is a fine ceremony, and though it may have been useful in the seventeenth century, is not a proceeding from which much good can now be expected. Whatever confidence may be placed in the decision of the Peers on an appeal arising out of ordinary litiga-

tion, it is certain that no man has the least confidence in their impartiality, when a great public functionary, charged with a great state crime, is brought to their bar. They are all politicians. There is hardly one
5 among them whose vote on an impeachment may not be confidently predicted before a witness has been examined; and, even if it were possible to rely on their justice, they would still be quite unfit to try such a cause as that of Hastings. They sit only during half
10 the year. They have to transact much legislative and much judicial business. The law-lords, whose advice is required to guide the unlearned majority, are employed daily in administering justice elsewhere. It is impossible, therefore, that during a busy session,
15 the Upper House should give more than a few days to an impeachment. To expect that their Lordships would give up partridge-shooting, in order to bring the greatest delinquent to speedy justice, or to relieve accused innocence by speedy acquittal, would be unreasonable
20 indeed. A well-constituted tribunal, sitting regularly six days in the week, and nine hours in the day, would have brought the trial of Hastings to a close in less than three months. The Lords had not finished their work in seven years.
25 The result ceased to be a matter of doubt, from the

time when the Lords resolved that they would be
guided by the rules of evidence which are received in
the inferior courts of the realm. Those rules, it is
well known, exclude much information which would
be quite sufficient to determine the conduct of any 5
reasonable man, in the most important transactions of
private life. These rules, at every assizes, save scores
of culprits whom judges, jury, and spectators firmly
believe to be guilty. But when those rules were
rigidly applied to offences committed many years 10
before, at the distance of many thousands of miles,
conviction was, of course, out of the question. We do
not blame the accused and his counsel for availing
themselves of every legal advantage in order to obtain
an acquittal. But it is clear that an acquittal so 15
obtained cannot be pleaded in bar of the judgment
of history.

Several attempts were made by the friends of Hastings to put a stop to the trial. In 1789 they proposed
a vote of censure upon Burke, for some violent lan- 20
guage which he had used respecting the death of
Nuncomar and the connection between Hastings and
Impey. Burke was then °unpopular in the last degree
both with the House and with the country. The
asperity and indecency of some expressions which he 25

had used during the debates on the Regency had annoyed even his warmest friends. The vote of censure was carried; and those who had moved it hoped that the managers would resign in disgust. Burke was 5 deeply hurt. But his zeal for what he considered as the cause of justice and mercy triumphed over his personal feelings. He received the censure of the House with dignity and meekness, and declared that no personal mortification or humiliation should induce him to 10 flinch from the sacred duty which he had undertaken.

In the following year the Parliament was dissolved; and the friends of Hastings entertained a hope that the new House of Commons might not be disposed to go on with the impeachment. They began by maintain- 15 ing that the whole proceeding was terminated by the dissolution. Defeated on this point, they made a direct motion that the impeachment should be dropped; but they were defeated by the combined forces of the Government and the Opposition. It was, however, resolved 20 that, for the sake of expedition, many of the articles should be withdrawn. In truth, had not some such measure been adopted, the trial would have lasted till the defendant was in his grave.

At length, in the spring of 1795, the decision was 25 pronounced; near eight years after Hastings had been brought by the Serjeant-at-arms of the Commons to the bar of the Lords. On the last day of this great procedure the public curiosity, long suspended, seemed to be revived. Anxiety about the judgment there could be none; for it had been fully ascertained that there was a great majority for the defendant. Nevertheless many wished to see the pageant, and the Hall was as much crowded as on the first day. But those who, having been present on the first day, now bore a part in the proceedings of the last, were few; and most of those few were altered men.

As Hastings himself said, the arraignment had taken place before one generation, and the judgment was pronounced by another. The spectator could not look at the woolsack, or at the red benches of the Peers, or at the green benches of the Commons, without seeing something that reminded him of the instability of all human things, of the instability of power and fame and life, of the more lamentable instability of friendship. The great seal was borne before Lord Loughborough, who, when the trial commenced, was a fierce opponent of Mr. Pitt's government, and who was now a member of that government, while Thurlow, who presided in the court when it first sat, estranged from all his old allies, sat scowling among the junior barons.

Of about a hundred and sixty nobles who walked in
the procession on the first day, sixty had been laid
in their family vaults.   Still more affecting must
have been the sight of the managers' box.   What
5 had become of that fair fellowship, so closely bound
together by public and private ties, so resplendent
with every talent and accomplishment?   It had been
scattered by calamities more bitter than the bitterness
of death.   The great chiefs were still living, and still
10 in the full vigor of their genius.   But their friendship
was at an end.   It had been violently and publicly
dissolved, with tears and stormy reproaches.   If
those men, once so dear to each other, were now
compelled to meet for the purpose of managing the
15 impeachment, they met as strangers whom public
business had brought together, and behaved to each
other with cold and distant civility.   Burke had in
his vortex whirled away Windham.   Fox had been
followed by Sheridan and Grey.

20   Only twenty-nine Peers voted.   Of these only six
found Hastings guilty on the charges relating to
Cheyte Sing and to the Begums.   On other charges,
the majority in his favor was still greater.   On some
he was unanimously absolved.   He was then called
25 to the bar, was informed from the woolsack that the

Lords had acquitted him, and was solemnly discharged. He bowed respectfully and retired.

We have said that the decision had been fully expected. It was also generally approved. At the commencement of the trial there had been a strong and indeed unreasonable feeling against Hastings. At the close of the trial there was a feeling equally strong and equally unreasonable in his favor. One cause of the change was, no doubt, what is commonly called the fickleness of the multitude, but what seems to us to be merely the general law of human nature. Both in individuals and in masses violent excitement is always followed by remission, and often by reaction. We are all inclined to depreciate whatever we have overpraised, and, on the other hand, to show undue indulgence where we have shown undue rigor. It was thus in the case of Hastings. The length of his trial, moreover, made him an object of compassion. It was thought, and not without reason, that, even if he was guilty, he was still an ill-used man, and that an impeachment of eight years was more than a sufficient punishment. It was also felt that, though, in the ordinary course of criminal law, a defendant is not allowed to set off his good actions against his crimes, a great political cause should be tried on different principles, and that a man who had governed an empire during thirteen years might have done some very reprehensible things, and yet might be on the whole deserving of rewards and honors rather than of fine and imprisonment. The press, an instrument neglected by the prosecutors, was used by Hastings and his friends with great effect. Every ship, too, that arrived from Madras or Bengal, brought a cuddy full of his admirers. Every gentleman from India spoke of the late Governor-General as having deserved better, and having been treated worse, than any man living. The effect of this testimony unanimously given by all persons who knew the East, was naturally very great. Retired members of the Indian services, civil and military, were settled in all corners of the kingdom. Each of them was, of course, in his own little circle, regarded as an oracle on an Indian question; and they were, with scarcely one exception, the zealous advocates of Hastings. It is to be added, that the numerous addresses to the late Governor-General, which his friends in Bengal obtained from the natives and transmitted to England, made a considerable impression. To these addresses we attach little or no importance. That Hastings was beloved by the people whom he governed is true; but the eulogies of pundits, zemin

dars, Mahommedan doctors, do not prove it to be true.
For an English collector or judge would have found
it easy to induce any native who could write to sign
a panegyric on the most odious ruler that ever was
in India. It was said that at Benares, the very place 5
at which the acts set forth in the first article of
impeachment had been committed, the natives had
erected a temple to Hastings; and this story excited
a strong sensation in England. Burke's observations
on the apotheosis were admirable. He saw no reason 10
for astonishment, he said, in the incident which had
been represented as so striking. He knew something
of the mythology of the Brahmins. He knew that
as they worshipped some gods from love, so they
worshipped others from fear. He knew that they 15
erected shrines, not only to the benignant deities of
light and plenty, but also to the fiends who preside
over smallpox and murder; nor did he at all dispute
the claim of Mr. Hastings to be admitted into such
a Pantheon. This reply has always struck us as one 20
of the finest that ever was made in Parliament. It is
a grave and forcible argument, decorated by the most
brilliant wit and fancy.

Hastings was, however, safe. But in every thing
except character, he would have been far better off if, 25

when first impeached, he had at once pleaded guilty, and paid a fine of fifty thousand pounds. He was a ruined man. The legal expenses of his defence had been enormous. The expenses which did not appear
5 in his attorney's bill were perhaps larger still. Great sums had been paid to Major Scott. Great sums had been laid out in bribing newspapers, rewarding pamphleteers, and circulating tracts. Burke, so early as 1790, declared in the House of Commons that twenty
10 thousand pounds had been employed in corrupting the press. It is certain that no controversial weapon, from the gravest reasoning to the coarsest ribaldry, was left unemployed. Logan defended the accused Governor with great ability in prose. For the lovers
15 of verse, the speeches of the managers were burlesqued in Simpkin's letters. It is, we are afraid, indisputable that Hastings stooped so low as to court the aid of that malignant and filthy baboon John Williams, who called himself °Anthony Pasquin. It was neces-
20 sary to subsidize such allies largely. The private hoards of Mrs. Hastings had disappeared. It is said that the banker to whom they had been intrusted had failed. Still if Hastings had practised strict economy he would, after all his losses, have had a moderate
25 competence; but in the management of his private

affairs he was imprudent. The dearest wish of his heart had always been to regain Daylesford. At length, in the very year in which his trial commenced, the wish was accomplished; and the domain, alienated more than seventy years before, returned to the descendant of its old lords. But the manor house was a ruin; and the grounds round it had, during many years, been utterly neglected. Hastings proceeded to build, to plant, to form a sheet of water, to excavate a grotto; and, before he was dismissed from the bar of the House of Lords, he had expended more than forty thousand pounds in adorning his seat.

The general feeling both of the Directors and of the proprietors of the East India Company was that he had great claims on them, that his services to them had been eminent, and that his misfortunes had been the effect of his zeal for their interest. His friends in Leadenhall Street proposed to reimburse him the costs of his trial, and to settle on him an annuity of five thousand pounds a year. But the consent of the Board of Control was necessary; and at the head of the Board of Control was Mr. Dundas, who had himself been a party to the impeachment, who had, on that account, been reviled with great bitterness by the adherents of Hastings, and who, therefore, was not in

o

a very complying mood. He refused to consent to
what the Directors suggested. The Directors remon-
strated. A long controversy followed. Hastings, in
the mean time, was reduced to such distress, that he
could hardly pay his weekly bills. At length a compromise was made. An annuity for life of four thousand pounds was settled on Hastings; and in order to
enable him to meet pressing demands, he was to receive
ten years' annuity in advance. The Company was
also permitted to lend him fifty thousand pounds, to
be repaid by instalments without interest. This relief,
though given in the most absurd manner, was sufficient to enable the retired Governor to live in comfort, and even in luxury, if he had been a skilful
manager. But he was careless and profuse, and was
more than once under the necessity of applying to the
Company for assistance, which was liberally given.

He had security and affluence, but not the power
and dignity which, when he landed from India, he had
reason to expect. He had then looked forward to a
coronet, a red riband, a seat at the Council Board,
an office at Whitehall. He was then only fifty-two,
and might hope for many years of bodily and mental
vigor. The case was widely different when he left the
bar of the Lords. He was now too old a man to turn

his mind to a new class of studies and duties. He had no chance of receiving any mark of royal favor while Mr. Pitt remained in power; and, when Mr. °Pitt retired, Hastings was approaching his seventieth year.

Once, and only once, after his acquittal, he interfered in politics; and that interference was not much to his honor. In 1804 he exerted himself strenuously to prevent Mr. °Addington, against whom Fox and Pitt had combined, from resigning the Treasury. It is difficult to believe that a man so able and energetic as Hastings can have thought that, when Bonaparte was at Boulogne with a great army, the defence of our island could safely be intrusted to a ministry which did not contain a single person whom flattery could describe as a great statesman. It is also certain that, on the important question which had raised Mr. Addington to power, and on which he differed from both Fox and Pitt, Hastings, as might have been expected, agreed with Fox and Pitt, and was decidedly opposed to Addington. Religious intolerance has never been the vice of the Indian service, and certainly was not the vice of Hastings. But Mr. Addington had treated him with marked favor. Fox had been a principal manager of the impeachment. To Pitt it was owing that there had been an impeachment; and Hastings, we fear, was on this occasion guided by personal considerations, rather than by a regard to the public interest.

The last twenty-four years of his life were chiefly passed at Daylesford. He amused himself with embellishing his grounds, riding fine Arab horses, fattening prize-cattle, and trying to rear Indian animals and vegetables in England. He sent for seeds of a very fine custard-apple, from the garden of what had once been his own villa, among the green hedgerows of Allipore. He tried also to naturalize in Worcestershire the delicious leechee, almost the only fruit of Bengal which deserves to be regretted even amidst the plenty of Covent Garden. The Mogul emperors, in the time of their greatness, had in vain attempted to introduce into Hindostan the goat of the table-land of Thibet, whose down supplies the looms of Cashmere with the materials of the finest shawls. Hastings tried, with no better fortune, to rear a breed at Daylesford; nor does he seem to have succeeded better with the cattle of Bootan, whose tails are in high esteem as the best fans for brushing away the mosquitoes.

Literature divided his attention with his conservatories and his menagerie. He had always loved books, and they were now necessary to him. Though not a poet, in any high sense of the word, he wrote neat and polished lines with great facility, and was fond of exercising this talent. Indeed, if we must speak out, he seems to have been more of a Trissotin than was to be expected from the powers of his mind, and from the great part which he had played in life. We are assured in these Memoirs that the first thing which he did in the morning was to write a copy of verses. When the family and guests assembled, the poem made its appearance as regularly as the eggs and rolls; and Mr. Gleig requires us to believe that, if from any accident Hastings came to the breakfast-table without one of his charming performances in his hand, the omission was felt by all as a grievous disappointment. Tastes differ widely. For ourselves, we must say that, however good the breakfasts at Daylesford may have been, — and we are assured that the tea was of the most aromatic flavor, and that neither tongue nor venison-pasty was wanting, — we should have thought the reckoning high if we had been forced to earn our repast by listening every day to a new madrigal or sonnet composed by our host. We are glad, however, that Mr. Gleig has preserved this little feature of character, though we think it by no

means a beauty. It is good to be often reminded of the inconsistency of human nature, and to learn to look without wonder or disgust on the weaknesses which are found in the strongest minds. Dionysius
5 in old times, Frederic in the last century, with capacity and vigor equal to the conduct of the greatest affairs, united all the little vanities and affectations of provincial blue-stockings. These great examples may console the admirers of Hastings for the affliction of
10 seeing him reduced to the level of the Hayleys and Sewards.

When Hastings had passed many years in retirement, and had long outlived the common age of men, he again became for a short time an object of general
15 attention. In 1813 the charter of the East India Company was renewed; and much discussion about Indian affairs took place in Parliament. It was determined to examine witnesses at the bar of the Commons; and Hastings was ordered to attend. He had
20 appeared at that bar once before. It was when he read his answer to the charges which Burke had laid on the table. Since that time twenty-seven years had elapsed; public feeling had undergone a complete change; the nation had now forgotten his faults, and
25 remembered only his services. The reappearance,

too, of a man who had been among the most distinguished of a generation that had passed away, who now belonged to history, and who seemed to have risen from the dead, could not but produce a solemn and pathetic effect. The Commons received him with acclamations, ordered a chair to be set for him, and, when he retired, rose and uncovered. There were, indeed, a few who did not sympathize with the general feeling. One or two of the managers of the impeachment were present. They sate in the same seats which they had occupied when they had been thanked for the services which they had rendered in Westminster Hall; for, by the courtesy of the House, a member who has been thanked in his place is considered as having a right always to occupy that place. These gentlemen were not disposed to admit that they had employed several of the best years of their lives in persecuting an innocent man. They accordingly kept their seats, and pulled their hats over their brows; but the exceptions only made the prevailing enthusiasm more remarkable. The Lords received the old man with similar tokens of respect. The University of Oxford conferred on him the degree of Doctor of Laws; and in the Sheldonian Theatre the undergraduates welcomed him with tumultuous cheering.

These marks of public esteem were soon followed
by marks of royal favor. Hastings was sworn of the
Privy Council, and was admitted to a long private
audience of the Prince Regent, who treated him very
5 graciously. When the Emperor of Russia and the
King of Prussia visited England, Hastings appeared
in their train both at Oxford and in the Guildhall of
London, and, though surrounded by a crowd of princes
and great warriors, was every where received with
10 marks of respect and admiration. He was presented by
the Prince Regent both to Alexander and to Frederic
William; and his Royal Highness went so far as to
declare in public that honors far higher than a seat in
the Privy Council were due, and would soon be paid,
15 to the man who had saved the British dominions
in Asia. Hastings now confidently expected a peerage; but from some unexplained cause, he was again
disappointed.

He lived about four years longer, in the enjoyment
20 of good spirits, of faculties not impaired to any painful or degrading extent, and of health such as is
rarely enjoyed by those who attain such an age. At
length, on the twenty-second of August 1818, in the
eighty-sixth year of his age, he met death with the
25 same tranquil and decorous fortitude which he had

opposed to all the trials of his various and eventful life.

With all his faults, — and they were neither few nor small, — only one cemetery was worthy to contain his remains. In that temple of silence and reconciliation where the enmities of twenty generations lie buried, in the Great Abbey which has during many ages afforded a quiet resting-place to those whose minds and bodies have been shattered by the contentions of the Great Hall, the dust of the illustrious accused should have mingled with the dust of the illustrious accusers. This was not to be. Yet the place of interment was not ill chosen. Behind the chancel of the parish church of Daylesford, in earth which already held the bones of many chiefs of the house of Hastings, was laid the coffin of the greatest man who has ever borne that ancient and widely extended name. On that very spot probably, fourscore years before, the little Warren, meanly clad and scantily fed, had played with the children of ploughmen. Even then his young mind had revolved plans which might be called romantic. Yet, however romantic, it is not likely that they had been so strange as the truth. Not only had the poor orphan retrieved the fallen fortunes of his line. Not only had he repurchased the old lands, and rebuilt the old dwelling. He had preserved and extended an empire. He had founded a polity. He had administered government and war with more than the capacity of Richelieu. He had patronized learning with the judicious liberality of Cosmo. He had been attacked by the most formidable combination of enemies that ever sought the destruction of a single victim; and over that combination, after a struggle of ten years, he had triumphed. He had at length gone down to his grave in the fulness of age, in peace, after so many troubles, in honor, after so much obloquy.

Those who look on his character without favor or malevolence will pronounce that, in the two great elements of all social virtue, in respect for the rights of others, and in sympathy for the sufferings of others, he was deficient. His principles were somewhat lax. His heart was somewhat hard. But though we cannot with truth describe him either as a righteous or as a merciful ruler, we cannot regard without admiration the amplitude and fertility of his intellect, his rare talents for command, for administration, and for controversy, his dauntless courage, his honorable poverty, his fervent zeal for the interests of the state, his noble equanimity, tried by both extremes of fortune, and never disturbed by either.

NOTES

THIS essay was first published in the *Edinburgh Review* in October, 1841, three years after Macaulay's return from India. It is nominally a review of a book that had appeared, *Memoirs of the Life of Warren Hastings, first Governor General of Bengal.* Compiled from Original Papers by the Rev. G. R. Gleig, M.A. 3 vols. London, 1841. Macaulay's opinion of Mr. Gleig's book, written to the editor of the *Review*, is, " I think the new *Life of Hastings* the worst book that I ever saw."

Throughout the essay, this opinion of Mr. Gleig's history keeps cropping out, in such passages as, " everybody believes, idiots and biographers excepted."

Macaulay's estimate of the importance of *Warren Hastings* as a subject was expressed to the editors of the *Review* when he was preparing to write the article.   He said he thought the subject would bear two articles.   He evidently decided when he began to write that the two parts would be better if combined. His original plan was to lay the first scene in India ; this he said would include the Rohilla war, disputes between Hastings and his council, the character of Francis, death of Nuncomar, rise of Hyder Ali, seizure of Benares, and so on.   The second scene would shift to Westminster ; this would take in the Coalition, the India Bill, and characters of all the noted men of the time from "Burke to Tony Pasquin."

Page 1, line 8. **uncovered.** Members of the House of Commons sit with their hats on ; to " uncover," or remove the hat, is a mark of honor.

Page 3, line 8. **renowned Chamberlain.** William, Lord Hastings, adherent of Edward IV., beheaded by Richard III.

> " Come, lead me to the block; bear him my head :
> They smile at me, who shortly shall be dead."
> SHAKESPEARE. — *Richard III.* III. 4. 107.

Line 21. The Hastings. Does not this sentence tell all the facts ? What do we gain by Macaulay's adding the following sentence ?

Line 23. mint at Oxford. At the time of the Civil War, Parliament held London. Oxford being in sympathy with the Cavaliers was made their headquarters. To Oxford, therefore, those who could not send money for the cause sent their plate to be converted into money.

Page 4, lines 8–11. **Living, tithes.** See Dictionary.

Page 6, line 16. **Churchill, Colman, Lloyd, Cumberland, Cowper,** all literary men of Hastings' time. Cowper is the only one of them whose work is still read.

Page 7, line 6. **Ouse.** Cowper lived with the Unwins at Olney on the Ouse. No life, in its environments, could form a stronger contrast with that of Hastings than his does.

Line 9. Temptations. Why does Macaulay tell us what Cowper was *not* called upon to withstand ?

Line 13. **innocence and greatness.** Is there anything unusual in the arrangement of the four nouns, "innocence and greatness," etc. ?

Page 8, line 3. **foundation.** A scholarship.

Line 7. **studentship.** At Christ Church College in Oxford, three scholars are elected each year from Westminster School. The scholarships are of the annual value of $400, and are to be held for two years.

Line 20. **hexameters and pentameters.** In England, the study of Latin is begun at eight years of age, and the boy of twelve must write as well as read in Latin. Proficiency in the language is judged, largely, by the ability to write Latin verse.

Line 21. **writership in the service of the East India Company.** In carrying on the business of the company, the **merchants,** senior and junior, conducted the trade ; the **factors** ordered the goods and attended to shipping them off ; the **writers** were the clerks and bookkeepers. By a kind of civil service, depending on worth and years in office, the writers could rise to merchants. The places where the company had their seats of trade were called **factories,** as the factories of Bombay, Madras, and Calcutta.

Line 22. **East India Company.** See *Introduction*.

Page 9, line 10. **Dupleix.** French governor of Pondicherry. In the *Introduction* there is bare mention of the events alluded to here because it is presupposed that Macaulay's *Lord Clive* has been read. Half of the interest of *Warren Hastings* will be lost unless *Lord Clive* is read first.

Line 12. **War of the Succession.** Succession to the authority of Asaf Jah, Viceroy of the Deccan, Nizam of the Carnatic. See essay on "Lord Clive," paragraphs 25-45.

Line 25. **the prince.** The Nabob of Bengal.

Page 10, line 23. **Black Hole of Calcutta.** When Surajah Dowlah attacked Calcutta in June, 1756, many of the English were able to get away on the river, but there were not boats enough for all. Those who remained defended the city until they were overpowered. When the Nabob, Surajah Dowlah, saw the prisoners, he promised them that they should not be hurt. The guards compelled one hundred and forty-six of them to enter a room twenty feet square. It had only two small windows, and they opened on an arcade. The heat and foul air were intolerable. At first the prisoners fought for places at the windows, and implored the guards for water, but later they taunted and insulted the guards in the hopes of making them shoot into the room and so end their agony. In the morning only twenty-three were alive. Surajah Dowlah may not have been responsible for this, but his later treatment of the survivors was not any more humane.

Page 11, line 7. **treason.** Meer Jaffier was a rival claimant for the Nabobship. When Clive arrived in Bengal he espoused Meer Jaffier's cause. Clive defeated Surajah Dowlah, Nabob of Bengal, at Plassey in 1757 and placed Meer Jaffier on the viceregal throne at Moorshedabad as Nabob of Bengal. The Great Mogul at Delhi was the nominal head, but the Nabob was really independent.

Page 12, line 3. **He remained at Moorshedabad.** What argument has Macaulay used to show Hastings' honesty at this time?

Line 9. **Mr. Vansittart.** Governor of Bengal from 1760 to 1764, between Clive's first and second governorships.

Page 13, line 24. **to marry a peer's daughter.** Would a simple statement, that the agent's sole object was to get rich so that he might return to England to enjoy life, be as effective as this sentence? Why?

Line 24. **rotten boroughs.** See *Life of Macaulay* in Introduction, and note on Old Sarum.

Page 14, line 7. **It is certain that.** What two devices of expression has Macaulay used from this to the end of the paragraph? Are they favorites with this master of style?

Line 16. **keen, severe, malevolent.** Discriminate between these words. In the following paragraph is there any relation between the words **squeamish** and **rapacious** that makes them good antonyms?

Page 15, line 10. **In 1764 Hastings returned to England.** This and the two following paragraphs begin with short, simple sentences. In what relation do the other sentences in the paragraphs stand to the beginning ones?

Page 16, line 19. **Hafiz and Ferdusi.** Classic Persian poets.

Page 17, line 24. **pagoda.** The word here means a gold coin which has a pagoda stamped on it. Value, $1.94.

Page 18, line 13. **Indiaman.** Name given to the ships for India. The voyage at this time was long. The ships went round the Cape of Good Hope. It took Clive a year to make his first voyage from England to India.

Page 19, line 6.   **genuine.**   What is the root of the word?

Page 21, line 16.   **There were two governments.**   At the battle of Baxar in 1764, Oude was taken from the Nabob Vizier. Clive on entering his second Governorship of India in 1765 restored Oude to the Nabob Vizier on condition of his paying half a million sterling.   Allahabad and Corah, provinces lying between the Ganges and Jumna rivers, were given to Shah Alam, the Great Mogul, on condition that they be used to protect Bengal from the Mahrattas; in return Shah Alam granted the fiscal administration of Bengal, Behar, and Orissa to the English.   The English were to collect all the revenues of these provinces, send about £300,000 as tribute to the Mogul, and give £600,000 to the Nabob of Bengal at Moorshedabad. But the political and judicial administration was left in the hands of the Nabob of Bengal.   In Indian terms the Company was **diwan,** and the Nabob was **nizam.**   This constituted the double system devised by Clive.   Even in carrying out the Company's part of this dual system, Clive did not put a servant of the Company in as collector of the revenues; instead he made a native, Mahommed Reza Khan, the minister of finance.

Page 22, line 8.   **Augustulus.**   The last Roman Emperor of the West.   See Roman history.   Analogous cases, because the real rulers pretended to bow to the nominal rulers.   **Merovingians.**   See history of France or Century Cyclopedia of Names.

Line 19.   **At present the Governor.**   Macaulay is describing the government of India at the time of this essay, 1841.   See *Pitt's Bill* in *Introduction.*   For present government, see *Introduction.*

Page 24, line 23. **important, lucrative, splendid.** Discriminate between meanings of the words.

Page 25, line 4. **Khan,** Persian, king.

Line 11. **Hindoo Brahmin.** See *Introduction.* The spelling in the *Introduction* is that in more common usage, Hindu Brahman. The great river of western India was originally the Ind or Hind or Indus; and the people are the people of the Indus, that is, the Hindus. Brahmin is from the name of the Hindu god, Brahma.

Line 14. **Maharajah.** Hind., Rajah, king, allied to Latin rex. Maharajah, great king. At the time that Clive chose Mahommed Reza Khan for minister, the Nabob had urged that Nuncomar be chosen; but Nuncomar had been suspected of treachery to the English in 1764 while he was Meer Jaffier's prime minister. Shortly after Clive had appointed Reza Khan, Nuncomar was imprisoned at Calcutta on discovery of proofs of his correspondence with Sujah Dowlah while that king was marching against the English at Behar. Both Clive and Hastings knew of his treachery.

Page 26, line 23. **sepoy.** A Hindu or Mohammedan soldier in the British army.

Page 27, line 16. **Mucius.** When Mucius was threatened with torture by Lars Porsenna he thrust his hand into the flame to show what a Roman could endure.

Line 18. **Algernon Sidney.** Convicted on insufficient evidence of complicity in the Rye House Plot. Died like a philosopher.

P

Page 29, line 22. **Directors.** The administration of the Company's affairs was in the hands of twenty-four Directors, elected annually by the Proprietors. The supreme control was in the Court of Proprietors, because they made all the laws and regulations and elected the Directors. The Courts of Directors regulated the commercial and political transactions of the Company, subject to interference by the Proprietors. It required the possession of £500 of the Company's stock to become a Proprietor, and £2000 of the Company's stock before a man could be chosen as a Director. The Crown at this time exercised no direct control ; but as many of the Proprietors and Directors were members of Parliament the interests of the Company were not neglected. The Regulating Act of 1773, and Pitt's India Bill of 1784, changed the constitution of the Company. See Mill and Wilson's *History of India*, Vol. III., Book IV., Chaps. I. and IX., and Vol. IV., Book V., Chap. IX.

Page 30, line 3. **Leadenhall Street.** The old India House was on Leadenhall Street, London.

Page 35, line 4. **Teviotdale.** See Scott's *Lay of Last Minstrel*. Scott gives motto of the Cranstouns in his explanation of the Cranstoun coat of arms.

Page 36, line 24. **sermons and rupees.** Is the figure strong ? A rupee looks like a silver half-dollar, and is worth about the same amount.

Page 37, line 11. **Corah and Allahabad.** For the agreement, see note on page 208. However, matters were now altered. The Great Mogul, Shah Alam, had fallen into the hands of the Mahrattas, the very enemies from which he had promised to protect the English through his possession of these two provinces, so there seems no reason why he should be allowed to keep the provinces or receive the promised revenue any longer. The revenue, Hastings asserted, would go straight to the Mahrattas if given to Shah Alam.

Line 21. **general dissolution.** See *Introduction*.

Line 25. **assumed the royal title.** In 1819, twenty years before this essay was written, the Nabob Vizier of Oude assumed the title of Shah, king. This province was loyal to the English, and was protected by them; but the Dowlahs grew tyrannical to their people and allowed their territory to lie uncultivated, so in 1856 Lord Dalhousie annexed Oude as a British province.

Page 39, line 15. **Ghizni.** English victory over the Afghans in 1839.

Line 24. **Rohillas.** Afghan Mohammedans who had settled in the foothills and mountains northwest of Oude. Like other Mohammedan tribes, they had sometimes fought with the Mahrattas and sometimes against them. Whatever may be said of Sujah Dowlah's plea that the Rohillas had not kept faith with him, Macaulay is surely right in saying that Hastings understood what would happen to the Rohillas when he left them at Sujah Dowlah's mercy.

Page 40, line 5. **Aurungzebe.** See *Introduction*, p. xlvi.

Page 48, line 2. **the Regulating Act.** An Act of Parliament in 1773 which gave greater political power to the Company, and changed the form of government in India. Its chief provisions are in the text.

Page 49, line 9. **Letters of Junius.** This was a series of letters against George III. and his friends, published in the *Public Advertiser*, on the political abuses of the time. They were brilliant and merciless. Their author very wisely and ingeniously kept his secret, so that it is not known even yet who wrote these letters. Macaulay loved to talk of the irresistible proofs for Francis. Carlyle once said, "As if it could matter the value of a brass farthing to any living human being who was the author of Junius." Is this Junius discussion a vital part of the essay?

Page 51, line 24. **Woodfall.** Printer of the Junius letters.

Page 52, line 6. **Doest thou well.** *Jonah*, chap. iv. 9.

Line 20. **Old Sarum.** This was one of the "rotten boroughs." It had been an important place, but had declined until it had not one inhabitant, yet the owner of the land sent two men to Parliament to represent it. **Leeds and Manchester** were two of the great manufacturing centres of recent growth that had not one member of Parliament.

Page 54, line 5. **Inns of Court.** See an article in the *Cosmopolitan*, March, 1900, *Where English Lawyers are made.*

Line 14. **twenty-one guns.** A salute for the president of the United States, a sovereign, a chief magistrate, or a member of a royal family. **Seventeen guns,** a salute for a viceroy, a governor-general, or a governor.

Page 55, line 13. **Bombay into confusion,** beginning of first Mahratta war in 1779. See *Introduction.*

Page 57, line 13. **Oates.** Titus Oates was an impostor who invented, in 1678, an alleged plot to kill the king, Charles II. Oates pretended to have discovered it, and on his testimony many innocent people were executed. When the excitement calmed down no proof of such a plot could be obtained. James II. had Oates publicly whipped "till the blood ran in rivulets" for his infamous perjury. Bedloe and Dangerfield were two of Oates' accomplices.

Page 59, line 11. **Munny Begum.** Begum, Mohammedan princess. Munny Begum, mother princess, or queen mother.

Page 60, line 18. **The triumph of Nuncomar.** Note the construction of this paragraph. What is the relation of the other sentences to the opening one?

Page 64, line 18. **superstitious Bengalees.** For this and other passages on Hindu castes and beliefs, see *Introduction*, and note on Benares.

Page 67, line 6. **holy waters.** Because the Hoogley is a mouth of the Ganges, the sacred river.

Line 25. **It is, therefore.** Do Macaulay's own premises here warrant his conclusion?

Page 70, line 1. **place-holder, place-hunter.** What are our American synonyms?

Page 71, line 12. **Jones's Persian Grammar.** Sir William Jones founded the Bengal Asiatic Society in 1784. He was the first English scholar to master Sanskrit, and to see its value in comparative philology. But it was on account of Hastings' minutes, to the effect that only through knowledge of the Hindu laws and religion could England hope to get a permanent hold on India, that strong encouragement was given at Oxford to the study of this, the oldest branch of the family to which our own language belongs.

Page 72, line 9. **Lord North.** Prime Minister of England from 1770 to 1782. Fortunately for the English in India, Lord North could not control Indian affairs in Parliament as he controlled American affairs there.

Page 78, line 22. **eighteen years before.** What date?

Page 79, line 7. **vigor and genius.** William Pitt, the elder, afterwards Lord Chatham. George the Third, in his determination to humble the Whigs, had succeeded in overthrowing the Pitt ministry in 1761, and the powers of Europe rejoiced at Pitt's downfall because his policy had been too wise and too strong to allow them to encroach on English liberties.

Page 79, line 17. **Calpe** and Abyla, the pillars of Hercules.

Page 80, line 5. **Mahrattas.** See *Introduction*, for all these names and the history involved.

Page 83, line 14. **a new danger.** Beginning of Hyder Ali trouble.

Page 84, line 5. **Lally.** Sir Eyre Coote commanded the English forces in 1760 at the battle of Wandiwash, and compelled the French to surrender Pondicherry, their last stronghold in India. Lally, who commanded the French forces, was afterwards tried in France on three charges — military misconduct, abuse of his fellow-servants, and pecuniary corruption.

He was condemned, and executed with unusual ignominy. Lally's son, ten years later, had this judgment annulled; and on appeal was granted a royal edict which set forth a high eulogium on the conduct and services of the elder Lally.

Line 23. **Porto Novo and Pollilore.** Names of places where Eyre Coote won victories when he was sent south by Hastings.

Page 88, line 1. **chambers that overlook the Thames.** See note on Inns of Court.

Line 8. **imported without modifications.** Macaulay understood this subject, for at the time of writing this passage he had completed his work with the India Law Commission.

Page 89, line 13. **the Company's territory.** What are the numerous devices used in this long paragraph to make it clear, vivid, and convincing?

Page 90, line 14. **alguazils (Arab.).** Police officers, constables. From same root as vizier.

Page 93, line 14. **rich, quiet, infamous.** A curious conjunction of words.

Page 97, line 6. **About thirty years before.** A periodic sentence is a device to excite interest by holding the reader in suspense. Is it possible to have a periodic paragraph?

Page 98, line 6. **Hyder Ali.** To understand the difficulties that beset Hastings at this time, the position of the various governments must be kept in mind. Bombay, Calcutta, and Madras were the three great English stations. Bombay had brought on a war between the English and the Mahrattas by

espousing one of the candidates for Peshwa. The brilliant
victories over the Mahrattas alluded to by Macaulay in a
previous paragraph won two of the Mahratta strongholds for
the British, but the great Mahratta Confederacy was not much
affected by them ; and Hindus, Mohammedans, and English all
knew that the Mahrattas were promptly ready to swoop down
on any or all of them if they showed weakness. Such were
the conditions surrounding Bombay. In the south Madras was
threatened by the Mohammedans of the Deccan and of Mysore.
In 1766 the Great Mogul had ceded a part of the Nizam of
Deccan's territory, called the Northern Circars, to the English,
when he ceded Bengal, Behar, and Orissa. But the Nizam of
the Deccan had declared his states independent of the Mogul's
empire, so that when the Madras government tried to take
possession of the Circars the Nizam called Hyder Ali to his
aid. A peace was patched up between the Nizam and the
English, but Hyder Ali was allowed to return to Mysore with
the understanding that the Nizam might make good his losses
by taking from Mysore. Hyder Ali quarrelled with the Nizam
of the Deccan, and the English at Madras did not aid the
Nizam, thus alienating him. Now, in 1780, Hyder Ali took up
his old grievance against the English, being assisted by the
French. The French had no hold on the mainland of India ;
but the French navy was to be feared. England had so many
quarrels on her hands, with America, France, Spain, and Ireland, that she could not send ships to protect the Indian coast.
The essay tells the result of this Hyder Ali war.

After Hastings left India, Tippoo, Hyder Ali's son, and the
Nizam combined against the English. This is called the second
Mysore war, 1790–1792. The third Mysore war, 1799, was

carried on by Tippoo. Tippoo was killed at Seringapatam; he fell fighting in a gateway with the last remnant of his body-guard about him. It was to the scenes of these battles that Macaulay was attracted when he went to Mysore. Tippoo Sultan's kingdom is now divided among the Feudatory States.

Page 100, line 4. **fling his guns into the tanks.** The tanks are reservoirs built by the English for irrigating purposes.

Page 102, line 16. **Benares.** Andre' Chevrillon, in his book of travels, *In India*, said of Benares: "This city is most extraordinary. Elsewhere religion is only a part of the public life; at Benares there is nothing else to be seen. It fills everything, occupying every moment of man's existence, and covering the city with temples. There are more than nineteen hundred of them, and the multitude of the chapels is past all counting. As to the idol population, it is nearly twice as numerous as the human, something like five hundred thousand. . . . each stone of it is holy. No pollution, no sin can endanger the man who dies within its walls. . . . In the morning when the throbbing disk of the sun rises behind the Ganges twenty-five thousand Brahmans, crouching on the river bank in the presence of the Hindu multitude, repeat the old Vedic hymns to the sun, to the divine river, the primitive powers, the visible sources of life. . . . Great patches of flowers are floating down the current; prayers without number are ascending to Siva, to Durga, to Ganesa, to Surya, the sun, which has become burning. In presence of the great river, among the pyramids of stone, under the colonnades of the chapels, at the foot of these huge edifices — strange as Indian vegetation and

Indian religion — swarms the infinite life of India. For a moment you seem to feel in yourself the overwhelming sensation which, repeated for generations, modifying the structure of the Aryan brain, has translated itself into their poems and their philosophies."

Page 103, line 22. **lords of Benares.** Mr. Wilson, in Mill and Wilson's *History of India*, says that Benares had at no time been an independent province. In the reign of the Great Mogul Aurungzebe it had been comprised in the province of Oude. In 1730 the zemindar, collector, of Benares obtained from Mohammed Shah at Delhi the right to adopt the title of Rajah ; but, though Rajah, he was still merely the zemindar of Benares, subject to the Nabob Vizier of Oude. When the English defeated the combined forces of the Nabob Vizier of Oude, the Nabob of Bengal, and the Mogul Shah Alam at Baxar, 1764, Benares offered to assume the same obligations for revenue to England as she had fulfilled to Oude, in return for British protection.

Page 105, line 4. **fall of the house of Tamerlane.** Tamer, the first of the Moguls.

Page 106, line 24. **a government** *de facto.* Can you not prove by running back over the text and the notes that not a single power, not even the British, was ruling both in fact and by legal right ?

Page 108, line 19. **Almost every question.** An obvious syllogism.

Page 119, line 14. **dotation,** dowry.

Page 126, line 22. **no connection between the Company.**
There was no connection until after Pitt's India Bill of 1784
had passed. The Ministry was not responsible, so the Opposition could not make an issue of Indian affairs ; but both parties
could denounce the chief actors.

Page 131, line 11. **Downing Street and Somerset House.**
Metonymies for the offices of the Exchequer, the Auditor, and
the Internal Revenue.

Page 135, line 1. **beneficent administration,** that of Sir
William Bentinck, Governor General from 1828 to 1835. See
last sentence of *Lord Clive.*

Line 19. **Pundits.** The learned men, or learned Brahmans.

Page 140, line 8. **zemindars.** Collectors of the revenue.

Line 11. **Carlton House.** Residence of the Prince of Wales.

Page 141, line 21. **Sir Charles Grandison.** An allusion to
the hero of an eight-volume novel of that name, written by
Samuel Richardson in 1753. Sir Charles, the hero, is an ideal
fine gentleman, whose manners are always most stately and
ceremonious. Macaulay was an insatiable novel reader. His
biographer gives lists of the classics of every land that Macaulay
had read and reread, but he tells us also the fun Macaulay and
his sister Hannah took in reading novels. Trevelyan says, " they
would debate the love affairs and social relations of their own
circle in a series of quotations from *Sir Charles Grandison* or
Evelina." One of their favorite pastimes was to annotate the
sentimental novels that were the fashion of their day, as —
" Number of fainting fits : Julia de Clifford eleven, Lady Dela-

more four, Lady Theodosia four," etc. These characters are all in one book, but not in *Sir Charles Grandison*. The hero, too, of this book is of a sensitive nature. " One of the sweetest smiles that ever animated the face of mortal now diffused itself over the countenance of Lord St. Orville as he fell at the feet of Julia in a death-like swoon." Macaulay thought he could rewrite the whole eight volumes of *Sir Charles* from memory. He certainly could have reproduced *Paradise Lost* and many of the foreign classics.

Page 148, line 5. **young minister.** William Pitt, the younger, was Prime Minister of England at twenty-five. See Macaulay's essay on him.

Page 149, line 22. **Brooks's.** A club-house. A Whig meeting place.

Page 150, line 23. **Edmund Burke.** These paragraphs show Macaulay's admiration for the great statesman, Edmund Burke. He once undertook a review of *Burke's Life and Writings* for the *Edinburgh Review*, but gave it up. He said : " It is a subject altogether unmanageable. There is no want of material. On the contrary facts and thoughts, both interesting and new, are abundant. But this very abundance bewilders me. The stage is too small for the actors."

Page 152, line 23. **Las Casas, or Clarkson.** Las Casas, a missionary in the West Indies and Mexico in the sixteenth century. Clarkson, a coworker with Wilberforce and Macaulay's father for the abolition of slavery in the West Indies.

Page 155, line 10. **streets of London.** In this paragraph Macaulay's skilful handling of form, color, and motion, and of

allusion, details, metaphors, metonymies, antitheses, strange things, and strange names, shows us the worth of specific words in descriptive writing.

Page 156, line 6. **Stamp Act.** All good Americans should read Burke's *American Taxation Speech* and his *Conciliation with the Colonies.*

Page 161, line 5. **sworn of the privy council.** Become a member of the Sovereign's council, which is composed of the great officers of the kingdom, the royal princes, the great judges, and other persons of rank and position.

Page 167, line 4. **First Lord of the Treasury, Chancellor.** Titles of members of the English Cabinet, or Ministry.

Line 19. **prorogation.** Parliament's annual sessions are usually from February to August. The prorogation is the act of adjournment for the annual recess.

Page 171, line 25 **High Court of Parliament.** The House of Commons must impeach, and the House of Lords must try the case.

Page 172, line 6. **hall of William Rufus.** This hall still stands, and is a part of the new House of Parliament. There is an illustrated article on this hall in *Harper's Monthly* for November, 1884.

Page 173, line 19. **Siddons.** Mrs. Siddons, the great actress, She was at the height of her fame at this time. Lady Macbeth was one of her favorite characters. Reynolds painted her as the Tragic Muse. Gainsborough's painting of her is in the National Gallery.

Line 22. **historian.** Edward Gibbon. *Decline and Fall of the Roman Empire.*

Page 174, line 2. **greatest painter and greatest scholar.** Sir Joshua Reynolds and Samuel Parr.

Line 14. **plighted his faith.** The Prince of Wales, afterwards George IV., was privately married to Mrs. Fitzherbert. It was contrary to law because she was a Roman Catholic. Royal Marriage Act, 1772.

Line 15. **Saint Cecilia.** Saint Cecilia is the special patron saint of music and musicians. Raphael and many later artists have given their conception of her. Dryden's *Ode to Saint Cecilia* and his ode *Alexander's Feast* were written for musical feasts in her honor. The legend of her martyrdom is well told in an illustrated article of *Harper's Monthly*, November, 1880. The allusion here is to Mrs. Richard Brinsley Sheridan, whom Reynolds painted in the character of Saint Cecilia.

Line 20. **Mrs. Montague,** who often entertained the members of the Literary Club — Burke, Goldsmith, Johnson, Reynolds, Garrick, etc.

Line 23. **Georgiana, Duchess of Devonshire.** The story runs that she bought at least one vote for Fox in his contest for Parliament in 1784 by a kiss. Her portraits by Gainsborough and Reynolds are very lovely.

Page 175, line 17. **Mens aequa in arduis.** A mind unmoved amid difficulties. In connection with this Macaulay says, " He was a man for whom nature had done much of what the stoic philosophy pretended, and only pretended, to do for its disciples. ' Mens aequa in arduis ' is his inscription under the picture in the Government House at Calcutta, and never was there a more appropriate motto."

Page 176, line 13. **bag**, bag-wig. A wig with a bag to hold the back hair, fashionable in the eighteenth century.

Line 25. **Fox.** Charles James Fox, 1749–1806, statesman and orator. Burke called him " the greatest debater the world ever saw." His is a very interesting biography. **Sheridan**, Richard Brinsley Sheridan, dramatist, orator, and statesman, 1751–1816, a brilliant speaker, as Macaulay shows. He is the author of the plays *The Rivals* and *School for Scandal*.

Page 178, line 2. **morning sun.** The sittings of Parliament are opened at 4 P. M., and often last till " morning sun."

Line 4. **Charles Earl Grey.** Earl Grey, a great Whig leader in Macaulay's own days in Parliament. Prime Minister when the Reform Bill of 1832 was carried.

Page 179, line 9. **taste and sensibility.** See previous note for the novels that fostered this " sensibility."

Page 185, line 23. **unpopular.** Burke did not believe in the French Revolution. He said, " Whenever a separation is made between liberty and justice, neither is safe." But he stood alone in Parliament. The Whigs followed Fox, and the Tories followed Pitt, in their approval of the Revolution. Later the country understood Burke's view, but it was too late to save the friendships of the great Whigs. Macaulay describes their attitudes toward each other in a subsequent paragraph.

Page 192, line 19. **Anthony Pasquin**, pasquinade, lampoon. Macaulay said of him, " The wretched Tony Pasquin, who first defended and then libelled him [Hastings]."

Page 195, l. 3. **Pitt retired.** Pitt, the younger, resigned the premiership because the king refused his consent to the removal of the remaining civil disabilities of the Roman Catholics.

Line 8. **Addington.** Prime Minister after Pitt resigned.

Line 9. **resigning the Treasury,** resigning the office of Prime Minister. The people regarded Mr. Addington as a weak and narrow-minded man.

INDEX TO NOTES

Q 225

Printed in the United States of America.